RELAX INTO
WEALTH

ALSO BY ALAN COHEN

BOOKS

Are You as Happy as Your Dog?

Dare to Be Yourself

A Deep Breath of Life

The Dragon Doesn't Live Here Anymore

Handle with Prayer

Happily Even After

Have You Hugged a Monster Today?

I Had It All the Time

Joy Is My Compass

Lifestyles of the Rich in Spirit

Looking in for Number One

Mr. Everit's Secret

My Father's Voice

The Peace That You Seek

Rising in Love

Setting the Seen

Why Your Life Sucks and What You Can Do About It

Wisdom of the Heart

CDs

Journey to the Center of the Heart

Living from the Heart

RELAX INTO WEALTH

HOW TO GET MORE BY DOING LESS

ALAN COHEN

JEREMY P. TARCHER / PENGUIN
a member of Penguin Group (USA) Inc.   New York

JEREMY P. TARCHER/PENGUIN
Published by the Penguin Group
Penguin Group (USA) Inc., 375 Hudson Street, New York, New York 10014, USA • Penguin
Group (Canada), 90 Eglinton Avenue East, Suite 700, Toronto, Ontario, M4P 2Y3, Canada
(a division of Pearson Penguin Canada Inc.) • Penguin Books Ltd, 80 Strand, London
WC2R 0RL, England • Penguin Ireland, 25 St Stephen's Green, Dublin 2, Ireland (a division of
Penguin Books Ltd) • Penguin Group (Australia), 250 Camberwell Road, Camberwell, Victoria
3124, Australia (a division of Pearson Australia Group Pty Ltd) • Penguin Books India Pvt Ltd,
11 Community Centre, Panchsheel Park, New Delhi–110 017, India • Penguin Group (NZ),
Cnr Airborne and Rosedale Roads, Albany, Auckland 1310, New Zealand (a division of Pearson
New Zealand Ltd) • Penguin Books (South Africa) (Pty) Ltd, 24 Sturdee Avenue, Rosebank,
Johannesburg 2196, South Africa

Penguin Books Ltd, Registered Offices: 80 Strand, London WC2R 0RL, England

Most Tarcher/Penguin books are available at special quantity discounts for bulk purchase for sales
promotions, premiums, fund-raising, and educational needs. Special books or book excerpts also
can be created to fit specific needs. For details, write Penguin Group (USA) Inc. Special Markets,
375 Hudson Street, New York, NY 10014.

ISBN 1-58542-563-X

Printed in the United States of America
10   9   8   7   6   5   4   3   2   1

BOOK DESIGN BY NICOLE LAROCHE

While the author has made every effort to provide accurate telephone numbers and Internet addresses at the time of publication, neither the publisher nor the author assumes any responsibility
for errors, or for changes that occur after publication. Further, the publisher does not have any control over and does not assume any responsibility for author or third-party websites or their content.

This publication is designed to provide accurate and authoritative information in regard to the subject matter covered. It is sold with the understanding that the publisher is not engaged in render-
ing legal, accounting, or other professional services. If you require legal advice or other expert
assistance, you should seek the services of a competent professional.

To the Dau family

Lodo, Romoto, Merelita, Luisa, Sio, Manu, and Paulina

for teaching me that real wealth

is of the spirit

INTRODUCTION

"Attention, ladies and gentlemen: I regret to inform you that the departure of flight 37 to San Francisco will be delayed due to mechanical problems. The new scheduled departure is two hours from now."

Aargh.

My first impulse was to head for the agent's desk to see if I could get my first-class upgrade request approved for the delayed flight. Maybe if I got in the agent's face, I could force it through.

By the time I reached the desk, however, a long line had formed; lots of other passengers had the same idea. I took my place in line and tried to estimate how long my wait would be. *Hmm.* Could be as much as an hour. A positive response was dubious. Do I really want to spend one of the two hours waiting in line for a probable "no"?

I remembered the lesson my seminar students report as being their all-time favorite: *Let it be easy. Struggle is not required.* If I were willing to let it be easy here and now, what would I do? The answer was obvious: I would head for the executive lounge and relax. If I got the upgrade, great. If not, okay. At least I would have spent one more hour of my life in peace.

I swerved out of line and headed for the lounge. I found a cushy chair, put my feet up, sipped some orange juice, read a magazine, and took a nap. Good call.

Fifteen minutes before the new departure, I made my way back to the gate to board. As I entered the departure area, I heard another announcement on the PA system: "Mr. Cohen, Mr. Alan Cohen, please come to the counter."

Now what? I approached the counter. Nearly everyone had boarded, so the coast was perfectly clear. When I identified myself, the agent cheerfully informed me, "Your upgrade came through."

Well, that was good news—and I didn't even have to stand there for an hour and go into my New Jersey act!

"This is really strange," the agent commented with a puzzled look. "I have no idea where this open seat came from. It wasn't here a minute ago."

Now we're talking. Tickled at the double pleasure of the hour of relaxation *and* the upgrade, I accepted my new boarding pass and gleefully moved toward the gate.

Along the way I realized that the agent hadn't collected the coupon payments due for the upgrade. Another *hmm.* Integrity. I returned to the desk and placed three coupons on the counter. "I think you forgot to collect these," I told the agent. She studied the computer another moment and came back, "Nope, the computer here says the seat is paid for, and that's good enough for me."

Now we're *really* talking. "Well, if it's good enough for you, it's good enough for me," I replied.

As I settled into my wide seat on the plane, I considered what had just happened—nothing short of a miracle. A magnificent demonstration of a principle I hold dear, which the universe was confirming to me firsthand, undeniably: *Relax, trust, and choose ease over struggle, and things will work out better than if you try to manipulate anxiously.* How much clearer could it get?

If you, like me, have been taught that the only way to get what you want is through combat, or to trudge through life playing catch-up ball, the book you are holding will assist you in making the crucial shift from an uphill-battle mentality to the deep knowing that you can have what you want without sacrificing your soul in the process. Success, wealth, and harmonious business relationships can be a lot easier than you have been taught, and here you will find many examples of how good it can get, along with practical tools to draw such experiences into your own life.

The stories and examples you read are the result of many years' experience experimenting with these principles in my own life, and seeing them demonstrated in the lives of thousands of seminar participants and coaching clients. They really work and they will work for you if you apply them.

Our journey will be illuminated by nine keystone principles, each introduced at the beginning of a section containing several chapters that illustrate it. Each key is accompanied by a shorthand memory-hook version of the principle for easy reference when you need it. At the end of the text you will find a summary of all nine keys, which I suggest you post on your desk, mirror, or somewhere that will remind you at just the right moment. If one or more of the principles speaks to you personally and directly, you might like to print out a larger version of it and post it on your computer monitor or dashboard. The more you remember and apply, the more rapid and powerful will be your results.

At the end of each chapter you will find a page of *Wealth Wisdom Builders*—several questions and exercises that will help you apply these lessons to your unique life. I suggest you do all of the exercises, either in writing or mentally, since personal activation is always more powerful than theoretical understanding. You will be even more stimulated if you go through the *Wealth Wisdom Builders* with your spouse or a friend. (I guarantee you will have some lively and enlightening discussions if you do!) Some of the questions are light and playful, while others are more probing. Just answer honestly and you will discover some very welcome insights.

At the end of each *Wealth Wisdom Builder* section you will find an affirmation. Each one can be a crucial asset on your journey to greater material and spiritual wealth. An affirmation is *not* an idea you repeat many times in the hopes of talking yourself into it and making it true. An affirmation is a statement that already *is* true, which you are helping yourself remember. Thinking or voicing an affirmation is like tapping an oil pipe into a reserve hidden deep within you. When you connect with it, you gain access to a vast resource which will energize you at the surface level of your life. You may strike riches with one repetition of the affirmation, or you may need to employ it many times before you find your treasure. When you do, you will know it. Something inside you will resonate, you will feel fantastic, and you will say, *"Ah—I get it!"* The best definition of an affirmation I know is: *The spirit within me loves to hear the truth about itself.*

I am excited about the possibilities for your life as you watch these truths work for you. If you progress even a bit—or a lot—from a sense of scarcity to one of abundance, this journey will be a milestone for you. And if you recognize that you can have all you want without torturing yourself to get it, that will be glorious. You might consider this book a representation of the airline upgrade I received only when I was willing to take care of myself and live the life I would choose rather than settle for. That same life is available to you, and nothing would make me happier than to know that you are living it.

—ALAN COHEN

CONTENTS

RELAX INTO WEALTH

ONE: ALWAYS ENOUGH

Abundance is natural.

EVERYTHING GIVEN,
NOTHING LOST

It's not a small world after all. . . .

As I turned the dimly lit corner, I stopped in my tracks and felt a chill of fear ripple through me. I clutched at my partner and gasped. Before me stood a massive, ugly, horribly mean-looking armadillo the size of a Volkswagen Beetle. If it attacked, there would be no contest, and vengeance would be taken for a hundred years of roadkill. But now we were the prey. . . .

I looked up at the sign above the armadillo's head: *True-to-size replica of prehistoric armadillo.*

Whoa.

We were not in the steamy jungles of South America, but the South Florida Museum. Apparently lots of stuff used to be a lot bigger than it is now.

Like the twelve-foot kangaroo. Or the dragonfly with a one-foot wingspan. Or flowers the size of your head. Or the Alaskan Tlingot tribe that crossed streams so packed with salmon that they could walk from one bank to the other simply by stepping over fish.

Some stuff is still really big and there's a lot of it. Scientists estimate 70 sextillion stars in the visible universe, in 125 billion galaxies. The most distant visible object in space is 15 billion light-years away from our planet. Thirteen billion gallons of water flow over Niagara Falls every day. Your heart beats 100,000 times a day. A giraffe can clean its own ear with a twenty-one-inch tongue. IBM scientists have developed a nanocarbon computer logic circuit, composed of a single molecule of carbon, operating on a material 100,000 times thinner than a human hair, and stronger than steel. There is even lots of big in little!

You don't have to board the starship *Enterprise,* safari in Africa, or take a microscopic voyage to recognize signs of a phenomenally abundant universe. How many blades of grass are in your lawn? How many leaves are on the oak tree? How many skeeters bug you when dusk hits your barbecue? How many cherry blossoms blanket Tokyo every spring? How much sand is on all the beaches of the world? How many cars are on L.A. freeways at rush hour? How many bytes fly around the Internet on a given day? How much is out there, and how much can we have?

Abundance

The answer is: *a lot, and a lot.*

While some of us may complain about how little there is of this and that, the universe was created in absolute, utter, glorious, eternal, nonstop, never-ending, over-the-top, knock-your-socks-off abundance. Not just enough. More than enough. Extravagant, actually.

Consider the mango tree in a valley near my house. When the fruit starts coming in June, my friends and I hike into the valley with a few penknives and old kitchen towels. We sit under the tree and feast on the mangoes—more than we could possibly eat. We look on the ground and see that for every mango we consumed, ten are rotting and returning to the earth. *That's* extravagant.

While our mothers judiciously impugned us not to waste anything because children are starving in India (where they are now answering your computer tech support and airline reservation calls), the universe has accomplished something absolutely stunning: it creates everything in phenomenal abundance and then recycles what is not used, to show up in a new form at a later date. Everything given, nothing lost.

That's efficiency.

Even cooler: perpetual abundance is ensured through a brilliant plan: Everything that exists contains the seed for its reproduction and proliferation ad infinitum. How many mangoes can one mango seed eventually produce? *An infinite number.* That's just one seed. *That's* vision and responsible planning.

If you will pardon my initial burst of enthusiastic flippancy, you will hopefully recognize that life is offering us all a great deal. Far more than most people realize and accept.

The intention of this book is simple and outrageously practical: to inspire you to recognize how much is out there, how much you can have, how much you deserve, and how much more easily you can obtain it than you have been told. If you capture even one piece of the equation, the others will fall in place.

And what about the children who really are starving in Asia? you may ask. And innocent people dying of AIDS in Africa? And the homeless sleeping on city steps while others walk past them on their way to nestle into cozy home theaters? And the rich and powerful who are dying inside of soul starvation? And if the universe is so abundant, why do you have to duck past your landlord's apartment at the beginning of each month? And why? And why?

My purpose is not to deny, minimize, or overlook physical, emotional, or financial starvation. It is to give you the keys to end it.

1. Sit right where you are or go to the window of your room. Name five things you can see that exist in great abundance right before you.

Sun, water, cloud, people, warmth from sun, trees, flowers

2. Mentally survey the world beyond your current view, such as your home, places you have visited, read, heard, or thought about, and photographs you have seen. What are the most abundant things you can think of? *Houses, cars, phones, computers, food, clothes*

3. Complete this sentence at least three times, with a different response each time:

> If I knew I lived in an abundant universe that supplies all my needs, I would _____.

AFFIRM:

I live in a universe of infinite abundance.
Life is capable of supplying me with everything I need.

ENOUGH ALREADY

When you realize that nothing is lacking,
the whole world belongs to you!

—Lao Tse

While I was having dinner with a best-selling author and speaker, our conversation came around to money. "I have enough money," he told me casually. "I don't really need any more."

My first thought was, "Well, sure you do—you make $20,000 a lecture!" After I got over my knee-jerk reaction, I had a profound realization: this man has enough money because he *decides* that what he has is enough. I had never before heard anyone say, "I have enough money." Most people I have met believe they do not have enough money. I know people who have millions of dollars, and it is not enough. I know others who have just a few dollars, and they are quite satisfied. I learned from this man that "enough" is not a number—it is a way of thinking, feeling, and seeing.

When Ted Turner donated a billion dollars to the United Nations, he proclaimed, "The world is awash with money." One could easily retort, "That's easy for you to say—you have billions of dollars!" But the question is: does Turner believe the world is filled with money because he has a lot of it, or does he have a lot of it because he believes it is available? The latter is the case.

The truly wealthy dwell in a consciousness of enoughness. Every thought you have falls into one of two streams of energy: *enough* or *not enough*. The more you observe and affirm *enough*, the more *enough* you have. The more you observe and affirm *not enough,* the more *not enough* you have. The author I dined with is not waiting to attain a particular level of wealth or prestige before he can relax. He chooses inner peace now. This makes him a powerful role model for his readers and students.

Contentment around wealth depends not on external events; it is the result of the vision you are using to view your life. At this moment you have the power to be rich right where you are, if you choose to be. If you complain about what you have or do not have, the universe takes you at your word and gives you more to complain about. If you celebrate what you have, the universe takes you at your word and gives you more to celebrate. The first step to building a wealthy bank account is to build a wealthy mind.

If you are struggling with finances, have lots of bills to pay, owe significantly, and cannot find a way to feel that you have enough money, turn your attention to other forms of abundance already present in your life. Money is just one thin slice of the great pie called prosperity. To deny that you are prosperous because of the numbers in your bank account is like negating the magnificence of a starry night sky because a small rain cloud is floating by.

Expand your sense of prosperity by focusing on the riches you already own. You can find wealth in good health; the beauty of nature; rewarding friendships; a loving family; bubbling creativity; your spiritual source; stimulating ideas; the kindness of people you meet; and much, much more. Right now in many ways you are a billionaire! You may be richer than many people with lots of money, because you give your attention to wealth rather than need.

The Bible tells us: "To him that hath, more shall be given; to him that hath not, more shall be taken away." At first this sounds like an unfair edict; why should the rich get richer and the poor get poorer? Yet this statement simply illuminates a principle of consciousness: energy goes where attention flows. Rich people think rich, and poor people think poor. The game is not about what you have; it is about how you are seeing it. Rich thoughts create riches and poor thoughts create poverty. Like electricity or gravity, the Law of Attraction is utterly impersonal and it does not play favorites. It is willing to fulfill its purpose no matter how you use it. Free will means that you are free to create your experience with your thoughts. You cannot change universal principles, but you can use them to your advantage once you understand how they work.

Does contentment mean that you must just stop where you are, never desire more, and never change anything from the way it is? If the door blows open on a cold winter night, are you supposed to just let snow pile up on your bed? Certainly not. A great way to position a contentment attitude is: *happy and hungry.* You appreciate what you have, and enjoy the adventure of expanding your world. You stretch and strive for better not because you are needy or greedy, but because growth and improvement are the nature of life. Everything wants to grow, and everything is perfect in its current stage of growth. Perfection is not a place you arrive at; it is an attitude you enjoy as you go.

A key step to struggle-free wealth is to align with the way that it is. There is always good right where you stand, and there is always a next level of good. Be fully what you are, and fully reach for more.

Enough for now.

1. What do you feel you have enough of?

2. What do you feel you do not have enough of?

3. Take a few moments to focus on the elements of your life that make you feel rich. How rich are you?

   How do you feel after you focus on your wealth?

4. Find within yourself the delicious balance of happy and hungry. What are you happy with? What are you hungry for? Notice how you feel when you let yourself be whole where you stand, while reaching for higher.

AFFIRM:

I am enough and I have enough.
I reach for more from a platform of passion and celebration.

TWO: YOU GET WHAT YOU LET

Life will give you as much as

you are open to receive.

MIND OVER MONEY

When I examine myself and my methods of thought, I come to the conclusion that the gift of fantasy has meant more to me than my talent for absorbing positive knowledge.

—Albert Einstein

Paul "Bear" Bryant, former coach of the University of Alabama Crimson Tide football team, led his teams to more victories than any other coach in college football history. His teams won an astounding 323 games out of 362 outings, plus six national championships. Under Bryant, Alabama was selected for bowl games twenty-four times. He is regarded as one of the greatest sports coaches of all time.

Bear Bryant had a coaching secret that was a pillar of his success: when he showed his team film footage of their games, Bryant focused on the plays they starred in. He did not show them films of their mistakes. As a result, the Crimson Tide just kept winning like no other team.

Coach Bryant understood that we get more of whatever we pay attention to. We learn from our mistakes, but the most powerful way to achieve a goal is to fixate on what you want to create. Look at a mistake just long enough to recognize it and stimulate your desire for what you want instead. Then turn your full attention to where you are headed.

The subconscious mind is the source of all that we manifest in the outer world. The inner pictures you hold and the feelings that accompany them form an energetic matrix that functions like a strong electromagnet. These internal energies draw unto you matching conditions in daily experience.

Your subconscious powerhouse does not distinguish between reality and imagination. If you can imagine something clearly, and get the feeling of already being or having it, the subconscious regards the experience as if it were real. This is why hypnotists can painlessly insert sharp needles through the skin of hypnotically anesthetized subjects. Hypnotized people also manifest blisters and numbness to *suggested* intense heat or cold; walk over 1,100-degree coals without being burned; and deliver impassioned speeches to large audiences when, under any other condition, they would suffer terrible stage fright. People with multiple personality disorders also demonstrate compelling mind over matter. One such person was severely allergic to citrus in one personality, breaking out in profuse hives; in another personality, he could eat half a dozen oranges without any symptoms. Another woman was diabetic in one personality, requiring her to take doses of insulin that would be lethal to her while in another personality. The subconscious mind is powerful indeed!

In our culture, the power of creative visioning has gone largely untapped and is even discouraged. In school, students are punished for fantasizing during class, while they could instead be taught how to use the faculty of imagination to achieve their goals. Psychologist Patricia Sun suggests that a period of time be set aside for creative daydreaming each school day. During this period, students would be encouraged to let their minds wander into realms stimulating their latent talents in writing, art, music, sports, or the trades. Students would enjoy the practice immensely, make significant advances in their field of interest, and demonstrate far fewer behavior problems.

Successful professionals often make use of creative visualization. A world-renowned concert pianist regularly sat in his seat on a train and practiced by visualizing placing his fingers on the proper keys. A basketball team mentally rehearsed making foul shots and increased its shooting average as much as a team that practiced physically. While prisoner David Marshall "Carbine" Williams sat in solitary confinement, he invented the Carbine rifle by drawing mental blueprints.

Most people have yet to recognize the intrinsic relationship between what we concentrate on and what subsequently occurs. Yet there are those, like Bear Bryant, who have latched onto the principle of imagineering, and achieve extraordinary success. The power of focused intention is equally available to you, and proves itself as you practice it.

The entrance to the theater of creative visioning is relaxation. You cannot imagineer if you are uptight, resistant, or stressed. When you let go of what is riling you, even for a few minutes, your subconscious mind leaps into action and begins to generate images that lead you from an unhealthy, unhappy, nonproductive position to a platform of high achievement and personal reward.

Doing is important, but holding a clear mental blueprint of your desired result is more crucial. (Ernest Hemingway advised: "Never mistake motion for action.") If your actions are not taking you where you want to go, it's time to step back and reevaluate the mental movies you are watching. If what you are doing isn't working, doing more of it will not work any better. Creative visualization requires far less effort than exasperated action, and sets you up to win. So quit spinning your wheels, shrug off the days' difficulties, and take a seat in the theater of your goals. Then you will be unbeatable.

20/20 Vision

1. What percentage of your time and energy do you spend thinking or talking about what you do not want or what is not working?

What percentage do you spend on what you want and what is working?

How do you think your life would change if you spent 10 percent more time and energy focusing on your desired results?

2. Who was the greatest teacher or coach you have ever known?

How did this person influence your life?

What did you learn from his or her teaching style?

3. Take a survey of the books, magazines, furniture, clothes, and artwork around your house. Notice how each object feels as you consider it. Does it lift you? Drag you down? Leave you feeling blah? Let go of what doesn't serve you, and fill your space with things that inspire you.

AFFIRM:

I create my life with my vision.
I focus on the positive, and the universe
delivers positive results to me.

OPPORTUNITY!

Sat 9/2/17

Do not wait to strike until the iron is hot;
but make it hot by striking.

—William B. Sprague

A round the turn of the twentieth century, a shoe manufacturer sent a representative to Africa to open up a market in that undeveloped continent. After exploring the culture for a month, the rep sent a telegram to the home office shouting, *"Disaster! Disaster! These people do not wear shoes. Bring me home immediately!"*

shoes

A short time later, another shoe company sent their agent to Africa for the same purpose. A month later his home office also received a telegram: *"Opportunity! Opportunity! These people do not wear shoes! Triple production immediately!"*

crisis = danger plus opportunity

Every situation contains the potential for disastrous problems or unprecedented success. The event is what we perceive it to be, and it will become what we make of it. The Chinese written character for *crisis* is composed of two other characters: *danger* plus *opportunity*.

No person, event, or experience is one thing only. Every situation is a blank slate upon which we project our beliefs, which create our entire life. It is rare that two people agree on exactly what reality is, because we are each generating our experience of reality with our ideas and expectations. Be wary of people who tell you, "Get real!" Usually they mean, "Get small!" What most people call "reality" is quite limited. Why hang out in a fishbowl when an entire ocean awaits?

No matter what direction you have been headed in, you can shift your course. A turn of one degree now will lead you to a far different locale a mile down the road. We are constantly molding and remolding our destiny with our ever-evolving thoughts. In the Bible we are told that we are created "in the image and likeness of God." We can use our minds, feelings, words, and actions to manufacture heaven or hell. At every moment we are already doing so, and at every moment we can make a new choice.

The story is told about a samurai warrior who went to a Zen master for training. "Please teach me about heaven and hell," the samurai requested.

"Me teach *you* about heaven and hell?" the master scoffed. "Look at you! You are a stupid buffoon! I wouldn't waste a moment trying to teach you!"

Upon hearing the master's insult, the samurai became furious. His face grew red and he began to breathe heavily. He reached for his sword and raised it to chop off the master's head.

At that moment the master lifted his hand and told the samurai, *"That,* sir, is hell."

Instantly the samurai realized he had created his own hell through his pride and anger. The teacher meant no harm; he sought only to awaken the student. The warrior was so overcome with the profundity of the lesson that he threw himself at the master's feet and thanked him profusely.

The master smiled and looked down at the samurai. Softly he told him, "And *that,* sir, is heaven."

Every situation contains a jewel if you know how to pluck it. While others may be wringing their hands and going in circles, you can find a quiet place inside you, put out feelers for the gift at hand, and move ahead far more easily and rapidly than if huffing and puffing with indignation. *You can make anything out of anything.* Why not make it what you want?

I met a woman who was developing her life coaching practice. A man came to her and asked if she would coach his son to improve his golf game. The coach considered this a rather menial goal, so she told the man, "I'm sorry, Mr. Woods, I won't be able to see your son. . . ."

Imagine that the universe is lining up to help you, delivering gifts to your door. But you must be open to recognize and receive the gifts when they are offered. Sometimes the gifts show up in disguise, in the form of challenges or non sequitur events. Resisting them spends far more energy than accepting the invitation. You will be amazed at how much less effort you have to exert, and how much energy you gain, when your question shifts from, "How can I get out of this?" to "How can I make this work on my behalf?"

If you are tired of the rat race and seek peace, reframe difficulties or novelties as opportunities. It's easier to flow than to fight. Flowing doesn't mean you never say no; it just means that you recognize where your yes lives and you move with it.

Reframe difficulties as opportunities
Make what you want!

1. In what situation(s) do you perceive frustration or failure?

What is the opportunity here?

2. In what situation(s) do you perceive threat or danger?

What is the opportunity here?

3. Who annoys you the most?

What can you thank this person for helping you to learn?

4. Are there any invitations or opportunities that you have been postponing or resisting?

What gift might be offered you?

AFFIRM:

I accept the gifts at hand.
I take what I have and I make what I want.

A PERFECT MATCH

When a web is begun, God gives the thread.
    —Inscribed on the ceiling of the Library of Congress

Fritz Kreisler was a gifted violinist who had a lifelong dream to own a Stradivarius. When he came to America, he took his life savings to New York City's music district and searched many stores. After numerous inquiries, he found a shop with a Stradivarius for sale. The shopkeeper went to the back of the store, removed the violin from under lock and key, and showed it to Fritz.

Fritz's eyes lit up and his heart began to pound as he held the delicate instrument to his neck and began to play. Heavenly tones sang forth, and Fritz knew this was indeed the instrument he had dreamed of. When he asked the owner the price, Fritz was shocked to learn it was twice the amount he had saved.

"Can we work out a payment plan?" asked Fritz hopefully. "Sorry, we don't do that," answered the shopkeeper. "Then will you hold the violin for me until I can borrow more money to purchase it?" "I'm afraid I cannot do that either, sir," the shopkeeper responded. "If someone comes in and offers the asking price, I will have to sell it to that customer."

Fritz went home and scurried to gather more money from friends and investors. He made slow progress, but within a month he found people to help him. Eagerly he returned to the music store and told the owner he was now able to make the purchase.

"I'm sorry, sir," the shopkeeper apologized. "You're just a little late. A few days ago a wealthy collector came in and purchased the Stradivarius."

Fritz was crestfallen. He had come so close to having his heart's desire! On his way out of the store, an idea occurred to him. He turned and asked the shopkeeper, "Would you give me the name of that collector? I will contact him directly and ask if he would sell to me."

The shopkeeper gave Fritz the information and he made an appointment to meet the owner. "It has been my lifelong dream to own this instrument," Fritz told the fellow. "Would you consider selling it to me? I think I can get some more money to purchase it from you at a profit."

The owner shook his head and answered, "I'd like to help you out, but I know the value of this violin. It is the jewel of my collection. I intend to keep it as an heirloom."

"I understand," answered Fritz. "Perhaps, then, you would let me play the violin for just a minute or two. It would mean a lot to me, and I will keep the memory for a lifetime."

The collector consented and handed Fritz the violin. Fritz took up the bow and, knowing he would never play this violin again, made the instrument sing with absolute passion. After a few minutes he returned the violin to its owner, thanked the man, and made his way to the door.

As Kreisler touched the doorknob, the owner called him back. "Don't go," he beseeched him. "You made such beautiful music. I bought this violin as a collector's item. You will bring more music and happiness to the world with it than I will. The violin belongs to you. Here, please take it."

Society's rules of ownership are superseded by a profound principle: the Right of Consciousness. You own what you own not by money, paper, or force, but by your love for it and your connection to it. If something is deeply imbedded in your soul, it belongs to you. It comes to you and adheres to you by your appreciation and right use of it.

While it appears that external rules govern who owns what, the prevailing law is the Right of Consciousness.

If you are trying to attract a job, living situation, or life partner, your thoughts and feelings must be a match to it. You must love it, know you deserve it, and hold a vision for healthy, joyful use of it. Then and only then will it come to you, and without struggle or strain. You don't have to fight for it; you just have to be one with it. If you are joined with something you truly deserve by your mental, emotional, and spiritual alignment with it, it is yours by universal law and no one can interfere.

A Course in Miracles asks you to remember, *I am under no laws but God's.* Behind all the rules people create, eternal principles are operating flawlessly. Justice is always being accomplished by the power of intention. Found yourself in universal principle, and everything you want and deserve will come to you and stay with you by virtue of love.

1. Describe a goal you have been struggling to attain or keep.

2. How does your struggle reflect your beliefs?

   Are you harboring any doubts that you really want it; whether or not you deserve it; or whether the universe can provide it?

3. How much do you love this goal, want it, and know it is right for you?

4. Why do you want it?

   Why do you deserve it?

5. Can you trust life to match you with your goal and help with the details of your rendezvous?

AFFIRM:

I line up my intention and the universe lines up the means.

I am equal to my dream.

WHY DON'T YOU JUST SELL IT?

If you will be clearly what you are,
the universe will give you clearly what you want.

—Abraham-Hicks

I was having difficulty selling a piece of real estate I owned. The property was a fine one, the market was moving, and the price was fair. Several potential buyers nibbled, but none followed through. I began to wonder what it would take to sell the parcel.

I told a friend about my dilemma and explained my various concerns about selling it. I wanted to find the right people to be my neighbors, get the right price, minimize taxes on the sale, and on and on. After I laid out all my doubts and considerations, my friend asked me point blank, "Why don't you just sell it?"

Her question hit me between the eyes. Yes, she was right. *Why don't I just sell it?* Suddenly I realized that the sale of the property did not depend on the many outside factors to which I had ascribed power. The sale of the property depended on me. I was letting all kinds of considerations distract me from my goal. If I chose to sell it, I could.

I realized that until that moment I had not been ready to let go of the property. I had allowed my emotional investment in it, along with the logistics of the sale process, to loom larger than the sale. Once I recognized that the only thing that stood between me and the sale was my own hesitation, I was truly ready to sell it.

Two months later, some dear friends, a couple, came to visit me. During a casual conversation the wife told me she had had a dream in which she was living on a meadowed hilltop in Hawaii with a magnificent panoramic view of the ocean. Hmmmm. "I have a piece of property that sounds like the one you're describing," I told her.

The next day, I showed my friends the property. The woman was ecstatic to behold her dream before her eyes. They asked me what price I would be happy to receive for the sale, and I told them. They said that sounded fine. The deal was done in about one minute, which must be a record in real estate.

Everything you experience reflects your intentions. When your sense of purpose is clear and strong, results show up quickly and easily. When you hold mixed intentions, doubts, fears, or resistance, the manifestation process becomes muddied and it takes longer to generate what you want.

Your journey to any goal is like driving a car. When you are aligned with your goal, your foot is fully on the accelerator. When you harbor thoughts or beliefs contrary to your objective, such as "I'm not sure if I really want this," or "I don't deserve this," or "the last time I tried this it didn't work," or "my life may change if I do this, and that is scary," you are stepping on the brake. If your resistance is mild, you will simply delay the manifestation. If it is strong, you may thwart it entirely. If you keep going back and forth mentally or emotionally, your car will lurch ahead in fits and starts, and your ride will be rocky.

Most people harbor mixed intentions around their goals. It is rare that someone simply knows what he or she wants, goes directly for it, and creates it instantly. When you bump up against mixed intentions, you have a valuable opportunity to decide what you really want and deepen your resolve to achieve it. As you face and move beyond your doubts, fears, and considerations, you gain clarity and strength. You recognize more clearly who you are and where you want to go. Then, as you line up your energy with your desires, you become very powerful indeed. Seen in this light, you can bless and appreciate the entire process, which is less about what is happening outside you and more about what is happening inside you.

I saw a T-shirt slogan that sums up this principle: *It's not how good you are; it's how bad you want it*. I would substitute the word *bad* with *much*. You can tell how much you want something by what you are getting. When you really want it and believe you deserve it, it will come. In the process, every arrow you shoot serves as target practice.

Wanting something dearly need not be a source of tension or frustration. It can be a source of rich empowerment. When you deeply desire a goal, it mobilizes a great deal of energy. When that energy hits a resistance within you, the collision is painful. If you can release your resistance even a little, that energy will move on your behalf. The game of success is less about *getting* good things to happen, and more about *letting* good things happen. At this moment a mighty river of energy is moving inside you toward your dreams. You have also constructed a dam of greater or lesser dimension that impedes the river. Open up even a tiny gate of the dam, and the river will begin to take you where you want to go.

A one-minute real estate deal? Done with a breath of allowance.

1. Is there something you want that you are having difficulty manifesting?

2. How might your difficulty be a reflection of mixed or contradictory intentions?

3. What payoff might you be receiving for not getting what you say you want?

4. How does confusion, disappointment, or failure contribute to creating what you want?

5. Complete this statement:

I am fully and wholeheartedly willing to receive _____ now.

Observe what happens inside you as you state this.

AFFIRM:

I set my intentions and life responds.
The more firmly I choose, the more powerful I become.

A RUN ON THE SPAS

Thought is the blossom; language the bud;
action the fruit behind it.

—Ralph Waldo Emerson

As I meandered through the hot tub store, a large aqua blue spa with a marbleized finish caught my eye. It was roomy and stylish, with lots of comfort controls and a back massager. This hot tub spoke to me like no other. "I like that one the best," I told the salesman. "Can you get it for me?"

"I can," he answered, shaking his head and laughing. "But it will take a few weeks."

"Why is that?" I asked.

"It's the strangest thing," he told me. "This model has been on the showroom floor for over a year. Until a few weeks ago, no one was interested in it. I tried various promotions, incentives for my salespeople, and various tricks of the trade to move it. It's a higher-end spa and we thought we might just be stuck with it or have to sell it at a loss.

"Then, two weeks ago, a couple walked in and bought the model. We were delighted. The next day someone else came in and ordered the same model. We were floored. Now here you are, interested in the same hot tub. I can't figure out what's going on!"

I knew exactly why this was happening: the Law of Attraction strikes again. The beliefs we hold create the results we manifest. When you develop a mental posture toward a situation, it tends to be confirmed and perpetuated until you change it. Then the new belief magnetizes more experiences like itself.

When the spa store owner and staff daily added to the bank of thought that this hot tub was not selling, it became unsellable, and their customers confirmed their expectation. An object at rest tends to remain at rest. Agreement is powerful; it can create the appearance of limits where there are none. When several people concur that a situation is fixed, it tends to stay that way.

When the sales staff's belief was dislodged by a customer whose enthusiasm about the spa was stronger than their doubt, the thought that the spa was worthy became their new belief, and that became the "truth," which attracted more of itself. An object in motion tends to stay in motion. When two or more people agree on greater possibilities, *they* become the reality.

This dynamic is often played out by couples who are trying to have a baby but can't. They attempt various fertility-enhancing therapies and methods, and every month when the woman finds she is not pregnant, the thought, energy, and vibration "no baby" becomes stronger and more real. Finally, the couple gives up trying to conceive and they adopt a child. Then, within a short time, the couple conceives a child of their own. This occurs because their concentration of thought and energy shifted from "no baby, no baby, no baby" to "baby, baby, baby."

In the cases of both spa and baby, someone in the outside world showed up as a focalizer of attention to a different result, which became the new "reality." Yet the spa salespeople and the parents might have quickened their manifestation by shifting their thoughts, feelings, and words *before* the spa purchaser or adopted child showed up. Through creative visualization, prayer, affirmation, or meditation, they might have repositioned their point of attraction without an outside agent providing them with a new object of attention.

At any given moment you are a reactor or a creator. (The letters that make up both of these words are the same; the same energy you use to react could as readily be used to create.) What do you focus on as the object of your creation? Do you allow your manifestations to be generated by what is happening around you, how you have historically thought, and how others have directed their energy? Or can you allow your world of inner vision to be so vital that your results proceed from your own choices?

At every moment you have the power to remold reality with your thoughts and intentions. When you sincerely set out to scribe a new course and you consciously focus your energy on it, there is a tipping point at which an old reality gives way to a new one. You tip the world not with a sledgehammer, but your thoughts. Archimedes said: "Give me one firm thought on which to stand, and I will move the earth."

If you keep bumping up against a recurring undesirable situation, withdraw your attention from what is not working and reinvest it in what you would like to work. Then you may find customers coming from all directions to buy the unsellable.

1. Have you given your power away to any external conditions?

   How have you let news, gossip, the opinions of others, the results others have gotten, or your past performance influence you to create similar results?

2. Describe a time when you refused to be influenced by the consciousness of others, and you maintained your truth and experience independent of external beliefs or conditions.

3 Explain in your own words the meaning of this phrase: *You cannot create in the experience of another, and another cannot create in your experience.*

AFFIRM:

> *My creations proceed from my own valued choices.*
> *I think, feel, and speak as if my heart's desires*
> *are possible, available, and already done.*

WISE INVESTMENTS

Capital can do nothing without brains to direct it.

—J. Ogden Armour

One Sunday morning, a hungry woman and her child came to the minister of a New York City church and asked him for help. Wanting to be of service, the minister gave her $25 to get some breakfast. After the church service, the woman returned and asked the minister for some more money, since she and her child were still hungry.

"What did you do with the money I gave you earlier?" he asked her.

"Oh, I don't have that anymore," she answered. "I bought some lottery tickets."

Money is not the answer to our prosperity problems. Wisdom is the answer. The only thing more valuable than money is knowing what to do with it. If someone does not know how to use money wisely, no amount of money will help them. If someone has a good money consciousness, they can take a tiny seed and grow it into a lush garden. If they have a poor money consciousness, they can take a huge gift and squander it in short order. Money is not the root of all evil; ignorance is.

This is not a book about getting money. There are lots of books and courses that offer you investment advice. This is a book about building consciousness. When you have a wealth mentality, wealth follows naturally. Money gained without consciousness will quickly return to the place it came from. Awareness is the steering wheel of your wealth and your life.

Studies show that many lottery winners' problems do not disappear when they collect their fortune; instead, they are magnified. Winners have to deal with relatives, friends, and ex-spouses wanting a piece of the action; suitors proposing to them with a hidden agenda; sudden radical changes in lifestyle; protecting their children from kidnapping; and on and on. If the winner's character and value system are not grounded and mature, the winnings can backfire in severe ways. (A number of lottery winners have committed suicide.) On the other hand, lottery winners who already had a good attitude about money and life tend to enjoy their winnings and help others. One financial analyst concluded: "If the winner was happy before they had money, they were happy with the money. If they were unhappy before the money, they were unhappy after the money."

There is a theory (which is much more than a theory) that if all the money in the world was redistributed so that everyone had an equal portion, within a short time the money would be back in (or out of) its original hands in the same proportions. (Studies also show that most lottery winners revert to their original level of prosperity within five to ten years.) So money is not a cause, but an effect. Mind is the cause; everything else is effect.

A friend of mine is a wealthy entrepreneur. He buys businesses that are falling apart, rebuilds them, and sells them at a handsome profit. When I asked him what he does for a living, he answered, "I channel money." The money he has is less significant than his ability to use it. The answer to prosperity issues is not to work harder; it's to work smarter. I find it fascinating that my friend takes businesses that others believed were impossible to resuscitate, and he finds ways to make them work. So the business was not a failure; it was the skill level or attitude of the owners that determined the results. Nothing is a failure unless you approach it with failure thinking. Shift your thinking to success, and you carry not an albatross, but a gold mine.

Perhaps you have heard about the South African farmer who could not make use of his land because it was too rocky and he could not plow the soil. He sold the property for a song to a fellow who saw greater value in the property. The buyer's name was Kimberly—of the world famous Kimberly Diamond Mine—the very property the farmer believed was useless. Behold the power of the kind of vision you are using as a key to recognizing potential.

Working smarter often means working lighter. When you are immersed in your work to the point that you have lost your perspective, it's time to step back and remember the big picture. I notice that after about an hour and a half of writing, my thoughts get fuzzy, not much gets put on the paper, and I feel tired. I used to try to force myself to keep going, but my results only diminished. Now when I reach that fatigue point I take a break. I step outside, have a snack, do some yoga, take a shower, or do something physical. Then when I return, I am back on the beam. The beam is always there, but I must manage my ability to be receptive to it.

Hustling more money may solve some of your cash flow issues temporarily, but focusing more astutely on what you are doing with the cash you already have can help you solve them permanently. Then you will not need to depend on the lottery to save you. Your wealth mentality will have already done the job.

1. What recurring pattern do you notice with your money?

What inner belief might this pattern be reflecting?

What is a more expansive belief you could nurture that would take you to the next level?

2. Think of people you know who constantly struggle over money or lose it.

How would you describe their attitude and beliefs?

What relationship do you see between how they think and what they are manifesting?

3. Think of people you know who are having fun with money and succeed consistently.

How would you describe their attitude and beliefs?

What relationship do you see between how they think and what they are manifesting?

4. Think of people you know who ask you for money or material support.

How can you be most helpful to them?

5. If you need money or material support, what besides cash might help you now?

THREE: PASSION PAYS

Do what brings you life.

DAD'S CHECKBOOK

Leap, and the net will appear.

—Julia Cameron

I feel caught between my old life and my new one," John confessed in our coaching session. He reached into his pocket, took out his wallet, and handed me his business card. It was loaded with telephone, cell, and pager numbers, along with several e-mail addresses and a Web site. "For many years I was very successful in the oil business," he explained. "I had vast amounts of money, prestige, and power. Then I got sick of the whole scene and quit. I just walked away from it all; I just wanted to clear my head and find some inner peace.

"I felt content for a while," John went on, "but then my money began to dry up and I started to panic. I had let go of all of my security and I felt like a trapeze artist flying through the air without a safety net. It was really scary. Then a few weeks ago, I received a phone call from a friend in the oil business, offering me a job. I don't want to go back, but I don't know how I am going to pay my bills."

I considered John's situation. "If you were not afraid about money, what would you be doing?" I asked him.

John's face softened and his eyes lit up. "I would study holistic healing," he told me. "I would travel. I would meditate. I would spend time in nature. I would connect with my spirit and pass along to others what I learned."

"Can you trust that if you are true to yourself, the universe will provide for you?" I asked.

John thought for quite a while. I could see he was moving through significant inner territory. Then he answered firmly, "Yes, I could." John's eyes looked resolute. He had tapped into a bank of faith.

"Then you are in a perfect position to manifest what you want," I told him.

A week later I received a phone call from John. He was laughing. "You're never going to believe what happened!" he exclaimed. "After our session I went to visit my father, who has never approved of my lifestyle. We had a good talk and I told him what I wanted to do. Without saying a word, my dad walked to his study and came back with a check for me. When I read the check I was stunned—it was enough to sustain me for a year."

During the next six months, John took yoga teachers' training, became certified as a hypnotherapist, and attended the Mastery Training. Then he went off to Nepal, where he meditated in a Tibetan monastery. Later, John came to visit me, and he bore no resemblance to the man who had been struggling. He looked happy. Then he returned to Nepal where, I am told, he is meditating peacefully.

The force of your personal evolution, speaking to you through your spirit, is moving you toward the fulfillment of your dreams. Your role is to move with the strongest energy you feel. If, out of fear or insecurity, you try to hold onto something that no longer serves you, you will feel constricted and unfulfilled. If, on the other hand, you give more power and attention to your destiny rather than your history, doors will open in amazing ways.

John had a strong intention to follow his dreams, but his fear was throwing up a thick smoke screen that obscured his vision. When he tapped into his faith, his fear dissipated. Fear and faith cannot coexist in the same mind or place. The antidote to fear is not to push hard against it or buck your way through it. The answer is to tap into a deeper knowing than the level that fear is speaking from. That deep place always exists inside you; your role is to relax into it.

There is a profound difference between fearlessness and courage. Fearlessness means that you are not afraid, so you go ahead and do what you want. Courage means that you feel fear, but you move ahead anyway. That movement is not accomplished through sheer will. It is accomplished through heart. The word *courage* derives from the French word *coeur,* which means "heart." So the answer to fear is not force; it is heart.

John's dad has a checkbook, and so does yours. Consider the universe your loving parent who is happy to support you to live the life you would sincerely choose. Then you will not have to make compromises and do something you detest. In the Sermon on the Mount, it is asked: "If a man's son asked him for a loaf of bread, would he give him a stone?" Just as you would answer your child's need, your spiritual source will answer yours. You can ask my friend John, but you might have to go to Nepal to find him.

1. Have you put aside any of your significant dreams because your known world feels safer?

   What would it take to dust off these dreams and put them into action?

2. Complete this sentence five times, with a different answer each time.

   If I were not afraid, I would _____.

3. Is there anything you have completed that you feel pulled to return to for safety?

   What do you think would happen if you tried to go back?

4. Where does your real security live?

AFFIRM:

> *I gracefully release my past and*
> *accept the possibilities available to me now.*
> *I step forward in faith, and my good comes to meet me.*

HOW TO KNOW
WHEN YOU'RE IN LOVE

Who looks outside, dreams. Who looks inside, awakens.

—Carl Jung

Dr. Norman Vincent Peale, author of the perennially popular book *The Power of Positive Thinking*, was seated on an airplane next to a young woman who struck up a conversation with him. When she discovered that Dr. Peale was a man of seasoned wisdom, she asked him for help with a dilemma.

"I have been dating two men and both have proposed to me," she explained. "I'm not sure which one to say yes to. Can you help me decide?"

"That's easy," Dr. Peale answered abruptly.

"Then tell me!" the woman eagerly requested.

"I don't think you should marry either of them," Dr. Peale stated authoritatively.

"Why is that?" she asked, surprised.

"If you have to ask me who to marry, you're not in love with either of them," he answered.

When something is right and good for you, it resonates within you in a compelling and unmistakable way. You know just because you know—not because anyone or anything outside you has convinced you. Your inner being speaks so loudly and clearly that you don't need confirmation or validation from the outer world.

If you want to know if a potential course of action is right for you, be honest about how you feel about it. If it feels like a fit for you, move with it. If it doesn't feel like a fit, don't act on it. If thinking about something doesn't feel good, doing it is not going to feel better. And if thinking about something feels good, doing it will probably feel even better.

Your guidance speaks to you in a way that is unique and meaningful for you. For some people, that knowing brings a sense of peace or relief, like hearing a familiar favorite song. Others feel tingly, bubbly, or experience a sense of exhilaration and increased life force. Still others feel a visceral sensation, such as goose bumps or the hairs on the back of their neck standing up.

Get to know how you personally experience your inner guidance, and then move with it. Practice doing only those things that match your joy, and avoiding deeds that grate against you. Make enthusiasm a prerequisite for action and you will progress to a new level of joy and success in your business and relationships.

If you do not know what choice to make, wait until you receive a stronger impression. Put the issue aside temporarily, ask for guidance from your inner sage, and keep listening and watching for signs. You might receive an insight in a dream; hear a key word from a friend; or receive a book recommendation that sounds interesting to you. Perhaps you'll see a magazine ad with a slogan that speaks to you directly. Or you could simply tap into a stronger feeling. Trust your knowing, however it arrives and expresses. Your answer may come immediately, or it might take a while. But it will come in the perfect way and time.

Other people can suggest, counsel, and guide, but their suggestions are worthwhile only if they resonate with your inner being. Try advice on for size, and accept only what fits you and enhances your life. Someone, something, some place inside you knows. Admit it, trust it, and act on it. You are inherently wise and lovingly guided.

We have been taught that we must search the world for answers, while they live within us. The story is told of the fabled musk deer that searches the mountains and valleys for the source of an exotic aroma. Eventually the deer discovers that the aroma is emanating from itself. Likewise, we do not need to struggle for guidance or spend a lot of time seeking advice. You may receive many opinions from well-meaning and qualified people. Yet since you are the one who must live with your choices, you must make them in accord with your heart.

Adopt the position recommended by Dr. Peale to the young woman: if you love it, you know it. If not, let it go and trust that your own shall find you.

Trust thyself: Every heart vibrates to that iron string.

—Ralph Waldo Emerson

1. Think of a time when you were asked to make a choice and you absolutely knew what to do.

   What was the situation?

   How did you feel or know what you were to do?

2. How does truth make itself known to you? (Peace of heart, tingling, warmth . . .)

3. Consider a decision you are being asked to make now.

   Which of the possible options feels most real and alive for you?

   Which could you act on with the most strength and confidence?

   Which would be most true to yourself?

AFFIRM:

> *My inner being always knows my best interests*
> *and guides me perfectly.*
> *I trust the truth in my heart, I open to receive it,*
> *and I act on it with confidence.*

WORTH IT

Self-loving is not so vile a sin, my liege, as self-neglecting.
—William Shakespeare

As we pulled up to the portico of the Beverly Hills Hotel, our rented Chevy Cavalier spoke a striking contrast to the array of Jaguars and Porsches lining the driveway. I turned to my musician friend Charley Thweatt and we laughed—this scene was right out of the movies.

The tuxedo-clad valet opened the door for Charley, who reached into his wallet and handed the fellow a five-dollar bill. Then we found our way to the meeting room where Charley and I presented a program for an early morning empowerment meeting.

After the gathering, Charley and I went to the hotel restaurant for some breakfast. We were not surprised to find that, like many exclusive restaurants, prices were not listed on the menu. (The assumption is that if you are eating here, you must be so wealthy that you don't care how much anything costs.) After Charley finished placing his order, he asked the waiter, "How much would a side order of bacon cost?"

"That would be five dollars, sir," the waiter answered respectfully.

Charley thought for a moment and answered, "I think I'll pass."

As the waiter walked away, Charley looked disappointed. He seemed to be pondering something quite seriously, but then his face lit up as if he had an "aha!" experience. "I just realized something very profound," Charley told me. "I had no trouble giving that valet five dollars as a tip for parking the car, but when it came to paying the same amount of money to feed myself something I really wanted, I hesitated to do so. I was more willing to help that valet than myself." Charley called the waiter back and ordered the bacon.

Many of us are more willing to nurture and support others than ourselves. It is easy for us to understand the needs of others and fulfill them where we can, but when it comes to meeting our own needs, we hold back. This imbalance is a call for greater self-honoring.

We are all familiar with the Golden Rule: "Love thy neighbor as thyself." But if you do not love yourself as much as your neighbor, you are not living the principle. If you were as kind to yourself as you are to others, you would find great peace and release.

While shopping with a friend, I found a shirt I liked. But when I looked at the price tag I put the shirt back on the rack. My friend picked the shirt back off the rack, handed it to me, and told me, "You're worth it." When I regarded the shirt as an expression of my worth, it took on a whole new meaning. I bought the shirt and enjoyed it for a long time; every time I wore it I remembered, "I am worth it."

While many people fear that following their joy is a sign of selfishness or egotism, they do not realize that they have a long way to go before they would become too self-indulgent. More people suffer from a sense of unworthiness than from arrogance. The remedy for unworthiness is practicing self-love. Consider every invitation that comes your way and every act you undertake an opportunity to feed your spirit. The items you purchase (or don't); the job you go to (or don't); the relationships you enter into (or don't), and the vacations you take (or don't) all demonstrate how much you value yourself and your heart's desires.

Consider the money you spend as an investment in yourself: you are buying stock in a company you believe in, you recognize your vast potential, and you want to get in on the ground floor of your achievements. I heard a woman report, "I love my husband so much that I would do just about anything if I knew it would make him happy."

Wouldn't it be powerful if you fell in love with yourself so deeply that you would do just about anything if you knew it would make *you* happy? This is precisely how much life loves you and wants you to nurture yourself. The deeper you love yourself, the more the universe will affirm your worth. Then you can enjoy a lifelong love affair that brings you the richest fulfillment from inside out.

1. What have you done for others that you would not do for yourself?

2. What would you like to do for yourself that you consider too self-indulgent?

Reframe your desire as an expression of your worth.

Now do it or make a plan to do it.

3. If you were to leave this world soon, is there anything you wish you had done?

What would it take for you to make it a reality?

AFFIRM:

I give myself as much love as those I care about deeply.

I am worth all that my heart desires, and more.

PAID TO BE
YOURSELF

Don't ask yourself what the world needs;
ask yourself what makes you come alive. And then go and do that.
Because what the world needs is people who have come alive.

—Harold Whitman

When Dave Barry was in junior high school, he was the class clown and often got into trouble for cracking jokes during lessons. One day, Dave's teacher scolded him: "You'd better get to work, Dave Barry—you can't joke your way through life, you know."

Now, over forty years later, Dave Barry is the most successful humor writer in America. With many popular books to his credit, he writes the most widely syndicated humor column in American newspapers. Oh, yes—along the way he won a Pulitzer Prize.

The junior high school teacher was way off the mark. Dave Barry *is* joking his way through life, and doing quite well at it. He is bringing laughter to millions of people, inviting them to lighten up about their difficulties, and inspiring all of us to live a more genuine life.

Likewise, the universe will pay you to be yourself. When you are true to what you love to do and what you do best, you pave the way to personal satisfaction, success, and service to others. Never allow the judgments of others to override your joy in being and expressing who you are.

Fearful people will give you all kinds of reasons why you should do the safe and accepted thing. They will tell you that a career in the arts is not lucrative; nag you to get that silly ring out of your navel; cajole you to take over the family business; pressure you to marry within the religion; and tempt you to worry about the same health problems that annoy them. If you pander to their fear, you will become like them—the living dead, or the fearful living. But if you stay true to the spark of enthusiasm that makes you feel happiest and most alive, life will reward you in miraculous ways.

What others tell you is wrong with you may be what is right with you. Small-minded people may label intense character traits as deficits, while they are really assets. When you honor your unique inclinations, they will guide you to your next step. A woman named Donna Lynn sensed that she had played out her executive job, and yearned for greater career fulfillment. One evening while working late, Donna Lynn visited the ladies' room and noticed that the night cleaning crew was throwing away toilet tissue rolls with a lot of paper left on them. Donna Lynn considered this to be a waste of a valuable resource, so she collected these rolls and took them to a local homeless shelter. Over time she found her involvement with this charity so rewarding that she became a volunteer, then a volunteer coordinator, and eventually went on to a salaried position as director of a citywide volunteer agency. Donna Lynn's work became so successful that she gained national prominence and received an outstanding service award that brought her to Washington, D.C., where she was honored by President and Mrs. Clinton and met several past U.S. presidents and their spouses. All as a result of a spontaneous thought about a roll of toilet paper! Some people might consider this concern frivolous, yet it led Donna Lynn to a rewarding new career, immense success, and meaningful community service.

The hardest thing in the world is to try to be something you are not, and the easiest to be yourself. This may sound too simple, but simplicity may be the perfect antidote for a complicated mind. As one sage noted:

"The truth is simple; if it were complicated, everyone would understand it." Never judge, minimize, or mitigate who you are or where you
feel guided to go. Never trust advice or opinions that ask you to be less
of what you are so you can be more of what others would have you be.
When you withhold yourself, you withhold all that you bring to life.
Aren't you glad Dave Barry didn't believe his critical teacher? She didn't
receive a Pulitzer Prize, but he did.

1. What character traits do people criticize you for?

   1.

   2.

   3.

2. What traits do you criticize yourself for?

   1.

   2.

   3.

3. How might these traits be an asset or service to others?

Trait	Asset or Service
1.	1.
2.	2.
3.	3.

4. Why do you think many geniuses and great people are considered eccentric?

5. Name someone who gets paid to do what you love to do.

   What do they know or live that you could learn from?

AFFIRM:

I celebrate my uniqueness and express it freely.

Life supports me to be myself.

MANY
HAPPY RETURNS

As soon as you trust yourself, you will know how to live.
—Johann Wolfgang von Goethe

I wrote my first book, *The Dragon Doesn't Live Here Anymore,* while I was living in a small rented attic. My only possessions were a tiny Honda Civic and a kindred guitar. I taught yoga in adult education school and earned just enough money to get by. I did my writing on a tiny electric typewriter I had borrowed from a friend.

One Saturday afternoon, while perusing a yard sale, I came across a typewriter similar to the one I had been using. It was priced at $50—a steep investment for me at that time. When I considered buying it, I rationalized that I didn't really need it; I was just writing for fun, and when I was done writing the book, I would just return the borrowed typewriter to its owner.

When I drove home, however, I could not get the typewriter off my mind. I sat down at my little desk and visualized the typewriter in front of me. Later, as I was falling asleep, its image popped into my mind. Hmmm . . . $50 . . . Was it really worth it?

By the end of the week, the thought of the typewriter was bugging me so much that I decided to go back to the house where I had seen it. If the typewriter was still there, I decided, it would be a sign from the universe. Sure enough, the yard sale was still going on (it was eternal). There was the typewriter. I bought it.

I finished my book on that typewriter, and *Dragon* went on to become a best seller. To date, it has sold over 200,000 copies. At the retail level, the book has earned nearly $2.5 million. Based on a $50 investment.

Since that time, I have written many more books that have generated significant revenue for publishers and me. Even more important, I have received many heartfelt letters from readers thanking me for inspiring them to change their lives for the better. Now I figure that $50 was a powerful investment in my work, my career, my life, and the world.

Like my typewriter, you may have a leap of faith before you now, symbolized by an action step you are deciding whether or not to take. You may hear about a class or conference; a home, car, or article may show up for sale; or someone may ask you to work with them in a new domain. You may feel moved to ask someone on a date, or for marriage, or to have a child. Or you may feel guided to end a relationship, job, or living situation.

Such leaps usually engender two strong feelings: excitement and fear. The question is, what is the balance of excitement versus fear? If your enthusiasm is greater than your reservation, you have the chemistry to move ahead. If you are more afraid than excited, keep examining your decision until you unveil your deepest knowing about it. The closer you come to your authentic truth, the more empowered you will feel in one direction or another.

You may hesitate to make an investment in yourself or a valued project because at the moment you do not realize its huge potential. You may wonder if the time, energy, or money is worth it. You may wonder if you are good enough. You may think that the person inviting you has made a mistake; that if they really knew who you are or what you can do, they would not be asking you. These are all issues of unworthiness the situation is helping you face and overcome.

While it may appear that your well-being hinges on your decision, there is a deeper purpose in the process. The invitation before you helps you focalize the issues around taking your next step. It assists you to recognize who you really are, how you feel, and what you want, and it forces you to tap into greater honesty and self-respect. In this sense, the outer decision is a template for inner growth. My decision to buy the typewriter was about far more than a typewriter. Did I believe in myself and my work? Was I worth having a valuable tool that would make my writing easier? Did I deserve to own my own asset rather than depending on that of another? And much more . . .

If an idea brings you delight to consider; if it is received well by others and they express an interest in hearing more; if it could uplift the lives of others; if you feel strongly moved to do it and cannot get it off your mind—these are indications of a worthy investment; not just in an object or situation—but in yourself.

Pray and ask for guidance about big decisions. Consult your inner being to feel if you can make this step with joy and confidence. If not, watch and wait. If so, leap. Look before you leap, but then leap. The investment may yield returns beyond your wildest dreams.

1. Describe a leap of faith you have taken and how it affected you and your life.

2. What step would be a leap of faith for you now?

Why do you want to do this?

Why do you deserve to do this?

What fears or reservations do you have about doing this?

What does your inner guidance tell you?

3. Is there some item or opportunity calling to you that represents making an investment in yourself?

How might this be a worthy investment?

AFFIRM:

My talents, visions, and intuitions deserve care and nurturing.
My choices represent my belief and my investment in myself.

CAN YOU *NOT* DO IT?

When the primal forces of nature tell you to do something,
don't quibble over details.

—From the movie *Field of Dreams*

For many years, my office assistant, Noel, had a dream of becoming a certified teacher. Noel often fantasized about going to a specialized school to take advanced training, but she was not certain if this was the correct path for her and she did not know how she would find the courage to accomplish it. Moreover, she would have to travel a great distance and take time away from her current work, friends, and family.

One morning, Noel arrived at the office glowing. "I have decided to go," she told me with a smile.

I could see she was quite resolute. "What made your mind up?" I asked her.

"I couldn't stop thinking about going. Finally last night I asked myself, 'Can you *not* go?' Then I realized that I couldn't *not* go. I've been thinking about taking this course for a long time, and the idea keeps knocking at the door of my mind. It only gets stronger. There must be a reason. I have heard that at the end of your life, it's not what you did that you regret—it's what you *didn't* do. I know I would regret not taking this course, so I called this morning and registered.

Noel traveled abroad, took her course, and received her license. She also met a man, got married, and now has a beautiful family. She is quite glad she followed her instincts!

Soon after I self-published *The Dragon Doesn't Live Here Anymore*, I wondered how to disseminate my book to the public. I knew nothing about the book industry, and I wasn't interested in the business aspects of publishing.

Then I came across the catalog of a distributor that specialized in books related to *A Course in Miracles*. I was a student of the Course, and a significant portion of the material in *Dragon* was inspired by the Course. This company might be a good venue, I thought. But since I was shy about self-promotion, I tossed the catalog into the wastebasket and put off my marketing plans for a later date.

A week later, I received a letter in the mail from a friend. When I opened the envelope, I found a copy of the exact catalog I had thrown away. "I think you should send your book to these people," my friend wrote.

Okay, okay, I can take a hint.

I contacted the company and showed the owner my book. He enthusiastically put *Dragon* into his catalog and placed sample copies in the hands of key people. Soon the book became popular. Before long I was receiving invitations to speak all over the world, meeting wonderful people, presenting programs, selling lots of books, and feeling more fulfilled in my career than ever before. In a short time my life changed in a huge way.

When something is right and important for you, the universe will stay after you, prodding you to do it. You may resist your next step, put it off, deny it, or even run away. But if an event, relationship, activity, or career is in line with your chosen destiny, it will find ways to get your attention and keep you in the game.

If you are not sure whether or not to do something, try *not* doing it and see what happens. If the impulse fades away, you have your answer. If, however, the voice becomes more insistent, or you can't stop thinking about it, or the universe keeps putting the idea "in your face," you would probably do well to heed its call.

Rather than judging or belittling your intuitive promptings, imagine they proceed from a source of wisdom. Most of the time you will find there was a good reason you were feeling the impulse. Your intuition is like a muscle; the more you use it, the stronger it grows, and the more easily you will recognize your joy path. Often you will receive confirmation by some kind of outer sign.

While I do not believe in a destiny that is forced upon us from some alien source, I do believe that we attract to us certain situations that we have chosen from a very deep level in order to advance us along our life path. Very often these situations keep presenting themselves until we acknowledge, receive, and act on them. If something keeps showing up and you keep wanting to do it, give it your serious consideration. If you can't *not* do it, you might as well surrender to love.

1. Can you remember a time when your inner voice kept after you until you did something that propelled you to a new level in your life?

How did your inner guidance get your attention, and what did you do to heed it?

2. Is there something you are feeling moved to do now, but have been resisting or procrastinating?

Is the feeling getting weaker or stronger?

If you were to heed its call, what would you do?

3. Do you have a spiritual practice that helps you attune to your inner wisdom?

When you are in touch with this guidance, what do you know?

AFFIRM:

I am open and receptive to the call of my chosen destiny.
I trust passion and enthusiasm to guide me to my greatest good.

HOW J.C. GOT
HIS PENNEYS

Truth creates money; lies destroy.

—Suze Orman

I met a fellow whose parents were friends of the fabled J.C. Penney, founder of the long-successful department store chain. When Dan was a child, Mr. Penney came to his parents' apartment to drop off a check for a fund-raiser. Dan remembers Mr. Penney telling his parents, "Well, I have to run now before the parking meter costs me an extra nickel."

I was stunned to hear that a man with such phenomenal wealth as J.C. Penney should be so concerned about an extra nickel's expenditure; I was even tempted to judge him as somewhat tightfisted. Upon further consideration, I realized that Penney obviously believed that no amount of money should be wasted. Because he had a system he believed in and he adhered to it, he accumulated vast wealth.

I later met a woman who had an unusual method of attracting money to pay her bills. On at least one occasion when she realized she did not have enough money in her checking account to meet her current obligations, she decided she would write the requested checks and trust that by the time the recipients cashed them, the money would be in her account to cover them. And her faith worked for her.

Behold two vastly opposite belief systems about how to deal with money—and both of them succeeded! There is a profound lesson here.

There are as many routes to riches as there are belief systems. Some people are quite frugal and others are quite generous. Who succeeds? Those who are true to their belief and expectation. A key element of prosperity is *integrity with your own truth*. If you act in alignment with what you know, you will succeed. If you try to succeed according to the formula of another, but do not fully understand or feel comfortable with it yourself, you will undermine your success.

Surveys indicate that the number one issue that most couples argue about is money. Such arguments often arise because the partners have different beliefs and styles about spending money. One person is typically a spender and one is a saver. The saver tries to get the spender to be more prudent, and the spender tries to get the saver to loosen up. When both partners are attached to their position—especially when fueled by fear or emotion—the argument goes in circles, no one wins, and nothing changes.

One of the ways to move the issue and relationship to the next level is for one or both partners to support the other to be true to their own beliefs. This can be difficult in a relationship in which the money is shared. Yet if one partner can relax and find space for the other partner to do it their way, some of the edge comes off the argument, and prosperity may be primed to flow more freely.

A client reported to me that she and her husband experienced ongoing angst about who handled the family finances. The wife generally oversaw the family ledger, and did so well. After a while she grew tired of the responsibility and resented her husband for not taking a part. Finally, she confronted him and asked him to take over doing the books, to which he agreed. It was not long, however, before she remembered why she was doing them: he was simply not good with money matters, and quite rapidly their financial accounting turned into a mess. So the wife took back the job, figuring that this was the only way it was going to get done—this time with greater understanding and surrender.

Prosperity—like a relationship and all of life—is founded on authenticity. When you are lined up with who you are and what you believe, things have a way of working out. When you try to sing someone else's song, you disappear and the universe will give you some very clear signs that you have strayed from your truth.

You don't have to explain, justify, or apologize for your belief system—you just have to live it. The way you live it may be entirely different than the way most people live, or anyone lives. It matters not. If you intend to build your empire by saving nickels, you will. If you trust that you will have the money to pay your bills by the time the checks are cashed, you will. (Just be sure that your faith is strong, or else you will get mixed results.)

What happens with your money is a perfect mirror of your mind. Use your financial interactions and their results as feedback on how true you are to your beliefs. In this sense, you can't get it wrong because you will learn from every event. Then you can rush to the meter or stay for a second helping of dessert, and you will win either way.

1. What style of saving, spending, or financial management (or absence thereof) works best for you?

2. Do you feel apologetic, defensive, or argumentative when someone with a different style questions or criticizes you?

3. Do you seek to impose your beliefs or style on anyone else?

   If so, how well does that work?

4. Name three people who are successful with money. Next to each name characterize their style:

Name	Style
1.	1.
2.	2.
3.	3.

5. Do you argue with your relationship partner about how to manage money?

   What keeps the argument in force?

   What eases it?

AFFIRM:

I am true to my beliefs about money and success.
The universe upholds me as I act in integrity unto myself.

UPGRADE

Take this step! Perform this act!
You will be astonished to feel that the effort accomplished,
instead of having exhausted your strength, has doubled it—
and that you already see more clearly
what you have to do next.

—Phillipe Vernier

As I spoke with Jana, who was thinking about signing up for the Mastery Training in Hawaii, she told me she was anxious about dipping into her savings to attend. "I have just a few thousand dollars, and this trip would deplete most of it."

"How is your life working?" I asked her.

"Not so well," she answered soberly. "I don't like my job, my health is not good, and I wish I had a relationship."

"It sounds like you have nothing to lose," I told her. As we explored her issues, Jana decided that anything she could do to improve her situation would be worth the investment, and she registered for the program.

At the training, Jana discovered her worth and experienced a huge energetic shift. On the final day of the seminar, Jana told me, "I phoned the airline to find out how much it would cost to upgrade to first class on my flight home."

"What did they tell you?" I asked.

"Eight hundred forty-two dollars," she answered. Then she added with an impish grin, "I told them I would take it." I was thrilled to see Jana putting the principles into practice by taking care of herself.

A few weeks later, I spoke to Jana on the telephone and asked how she enjoyed her flight home. "I *loved* first class," she told me. "I stayed up all night on the overnight flight, leisurely sipping free cocktails and wiggling from side to side in the wide seat. I think I will fly first class from now on!"

Jana went on: "When I arrived home, I experienced a miracle. I discovered I had a pension fund I had entirely forgotten about, with a balance of several thousand dollars. So my trip was entirely paid for, including my first-class upgrade!"

When you are thinking about doing something that stretches you financially, do not think of the money as a loss; instead, consider it an affirmation of your worth or that of your project. Many years ago, Louise Hay wrote a small pamphlet called *Heal Your Body*, mapping the relationship between patterns of thought, disease, and healing. The booklet became popular and Louise decided to mass-produce the next edition herself. She had the pages printed by a local printer and then she stapled them together, with the help of her mother. One evening as the two were sitting on Louise's living room floor stapling pamphlets, her mom suggested, "Why don't you get an electric stapler, dear?"

"Oh, that would cost seventy-five dollars, Mom," Louise answered. "I don't know if I could afford it."

But when Louise thought about it, she decided this would be a perfect opportunity to practice the principles she was teaching. She bought an electric stapler, and the rest is history. Louise's pamphlet grew into the book *You Can Heal Your Life*, which became an international best seller. Louise's publishing company, Hay House, has grown to be a significant force in the holistic health field, publishing major authors and earning many millions of dollars annually. When I last visited Louise, she took me out to lunch in her gold Rolls-Royce.

While some religions and spiritual paths suggest that you should slice away desire and be content with whatever comes your way, I be-

lieve that life is more about expansion than settling. Your desire for a
better life is not a sign of greed, but natural growth. The current of evolution keeps moving life to more sophisticated and joyful levels.

Louise Hay is hurting no one by having a Rolls-Royce, and you
hurt no one by seeking and claiming better for yourself. That better
may take the form of a first-class seat on an airplane, a home in an area
that speaks to you, or a relationship with more depth and connection.
Your upgrade may also move you to greater simplicity in your life;
most people who have a lot of stuff get to a point where they would
prefer to lighten up. The key factor is not what you want, but why you
want it. If your life as it is is a match to your true self and your true
choices, then carry on in high style. If there is something next, ask for
it and claim it. Jana ended up with her first-class seat as well as the
money it cost her for it. Not a bad deal, after all.

1. What percentage of your annual expenditures do you devote to fun, celebration, and self-care?

Would you be willing to increase this percentage? To how much?

2. Of all the money you have ever spent, what investments in yourself do you most remember?

3. If you were given a large sum of money with the stipulation that you invest it only in acts or objects of joy, self-expression, or creativity, what would you do with it?

Would you consider investing some of your money in self-honoring now, with faith it will be rewarded?

4. If you had more money to support other people in their joy, who would you help and what would you help them do or get?

AFFIRM:

I move gracefully from good to better to best.
I ask for all of what I want, and the universe responds.

FOUR: DON'T SWEAT THE PETTY STUFF AND DON'T PET THE SWEATY STUFF

Let it be easy.

Struggle is not required.

WHAT GOES AROUND

I have always found that mercy bears richer fruits
than strict justice.

—Abraham Lincoln

Many years ago I presented an evening seminar at a holistic health center. We had a large attendance, and at the end of the evening the sponsor gave me a check for over $1,000. After I deposited the check, it was returned for insufficient funds. When I tried to deposit the check again, I was told that the sponsor's account had been closed.

I called the sponsor and asked her what was happening. She explained that the center was going bankrupt, but she would make good on the check. A few weeks later, I received a letter from her telling me that her accountant had advised her that she would be able to pay the bill over a period of about three years.

I thought about the issue and decided not to try to force it. I did not want to spend the time, energy, and angst chasing her around for the money. So I let the issue go for the time being. As months went by, however, the debt bothered me and I felt irritated when I thought about it. After a year went by, I sent the sponsor a friendly letter asking her if she was able to pay. She told me that she was still struggling financially. Another year went by and still I received no payment. I sent another letter and received no response.

Then, while paging through a magazine, I discovered that the same woman had opened another center and she was sponsoring workshops. Apparently, the center was doing well and she was obviously reaping an income. Clearly, she was in a position to pay me now.

Irritated, I drafted a strong letter to this woman, putting pressure on her to pay up. I finished the letter on the day I was leaving for a lecture tour, and advised my assistant to hold it for a few days until I gave the matter final consideration.

During the tour I prayed about the issue. My inner guidance said to just release it. Trying to extract money from this woman would be no easy task, and certainly no fun. I realized that my sense of being ripped off had ripped me off subtly over three years, and I did not want to lose any more peace about it. I felt a lot lighter and freer to just forget about the debt and get on with my life. I called my assistant and told him to tear up the letter.

That week, I presented a program to a large group for which I was to be paid according to the number of people who attended. I counted the audience and determined that my income for the event would be roughly $3,000. At the end of the program, the sponsor handed me a check for $4,000. I asked him if that was accurate, and he said he was sure it was.

Then I laughed. The universe was showing me how things come around. In one sector I took a surprise loss, but in another sector I received a surprise gain of equal value. The unexpected gift made the income even more meaningful to me. I realized that my idea of justice was much too small. The universe has clever ways of reconciling imbalances. The money I had "lost" on the first event came back through another door.

What goes around comes around. Life has a way of settling accounts. We are playing on a field much larger than we recognize. In the long run, it doesn't matter how accounts are settled. Just trust that everything will be taken care of.

Fighting over money usually takes more effort and energy than it is worth. How much is money worth to you? Is it worth your happiness? Your peace? Your health? Your relationships? Your life? If you are tempted to threaten or punish others over money, ask yourself if strong-arm tactics are really worth it. Is this going to bring you what you really want? If you trusted in your well-being and life's willingness and ability to provide it, would you be investing your time and energy in this, or are there other more enjoyable things you would rather be doing?

Ask for what you want and deserve, and ask those with whom you interact to be responsible about their agreements. Give integrity and request it. Yet keep your transactions in perspective. *The main thing is to keep the main thing the main thing.* Keep inner peace first, and your books will balance in profound and even miraculous ways.

The tide always comes in again.

—Dr. Norman Vincent Peale

1. Are you fighting with anyone over money?

   Have you lost your peace in the process?

   If you kept inner peace as your highest priority, what would you be doing differently?

2. How does focusing on past debts keep you from living fully in the present?

3. If you knew that life would take care of you no matter what temporary setbacks occur, how would you be feeling or acting differently?

4. Can you think of a time when you let go of something that was troubling you, and an unexpected solution arose?

AFFIRM:

Life takes care of me in miraculous ways.
I let go of any sense of loss and accept my good
through clever doors and packages.

SURFING JAWS

Success doesn't have to pull, tug, or chafe if we wear our real size.
—Sarah Ben Breathnach

Just a few miles from my home is a world-famous surfing cove known as Jaws. This rugged bay is so named for some of the largest waves in the world. At the height of winter, only the most skilled and die-hard surfers go out to ride monster waves as high as seventy feet. The waves are so gigantic that the surfers must be towed out past the break on Jet Skis so they can build up speed to catch the mammoth surf.

I saw the motion picture *In God's Hands,* which was filmed at Jaws, and was astounded to watch the king of the surfers ride a huge wave that made him look like a toothpick by comparison. I was even more amazed that he looked really *relaxed,* as he had poise and balance even as he negotiated a wave the size of a three-story building. Then I understood: *relaxation is more powerful than resistance.* He was not relaxed because he was the king. He was the king because he was able to stay relaxed in the most trying of circumstances.

The telling feature of a true master is poise. As you maintain grace under fire, you emerge triumphant. Any form of anxiety-motivated defensiveness or pushing against people or conditions will only weaken you and make you vulnerable. Stay balanced as you stand firmly for your intention, and you will be aligned with the Force, which is unstoppable.

When I first began to organize and present personal and professional development retreats, I did so quite nervously. At the outset of a program I ran around like a headless chicken, making sure all the details were covered. I probably wasn't a good model of ease.

Then I went to a large convention at a major university, attended by several thousand participants. On the first evening of the program, I observed the program director chatting with some participants in the courtyard. To my amazement, he was quite relaxed, laughing with his clients, and obviously having a really good time. That image affected me profoundly. If he could be at ease and playful with a responsibility for thousands of people, I figured I could be relaxed with a responsibility for far fewer. That is exactly the posture into which I evolved. One moment of observing that positive role model has made a huge difference in my life and my work.

Sometimes a challenging experience or an adventure that stretches you brings you a benefit that is not obvious at the moment, but bears fruit over time. One of my clients lost his job as an entertainer and sought a new one over two years' time. This period was quite trying for Jerome, for his self-esteem was tied up in his performance and the approval of others. In our coaching it became apparent to both of us that Jerome had given his power away to his role, and much of his life's reward had depended on other people's opinion of him. His jobless time afforded him the tremendous opportunity to recognize his worth not for what he does but for who he is. Though difficult at first, the lesson eventually sank in and Jerome developed a sense of self-acceptance and self-respect that he never would have enjoyed if he continued to let other people be the source of his validation. When he finally returned to the workforce, he had grown and solidified so much that he was like a new person, his performance was far superior to what it had been, and, most important, he bore a sense of wholeness he had previously not owned.

You are simultaneously on two journeys. One is a horizontal journey represented by the story line of your life: events, encounters, experiences, relationships, and outcomes. The other is a vertical journey represented by what is going on inside you: joy, sorrow, peace, frustration, numbness, or aliveness. While most people believe and act as if the horizontal journey is their purpose in living, in truth we are here for the vertical journey. Behind all of your worldly exploits, you are a spiritual being here to unfold to your highest personal reward and expression. If you get hung up on the outer journey but do not recognize the inner one, you will be lost and confused in a big game of Chutes and Ladders that has no meaning or direction. If you check in with your inner self often and make course corrections in the direction of authenticity and joy, you will stay on track and your life will have meaning, purpose, and reward.

Your life is less about what you are doing and more about how you are doing it. That is why some people in lowly positions are soaring spiritually while many in esteemed positions are soul-starved. If, when you surf your personal Jaws, you can maintain a sense of flow, poise, and integrity, you are truly a success. Reframe any Jaws you come up against not as bad luck or punishment, but an opportunity to rise in your vertical journey. Then you will find yourself on shore perhaps with a trophy from the world, but more important with the knowledge that you stayed true to the real ride you signed up for.

You don't have to stay up nights to succeed;
you have to stay awake days.

—Source unknown

1. Describe an event in your past that seemed overwhelming when it occurred, but ultimately empowered you.

What shift in consciousness enabled you to generate the transformation?

2. Is there anything happening around you now that seems overwhelming?

If so, how can you see it or respond to it in a way that serves you?

3. Where are you currently on your horizontal journey?

Where are you on your vertical journey?

How can you accelerate your movement on your vertical journey?

AFFIRM:

I move gracefully from my center.
I harmonize with the forces in and around me,
and harness energy to my advantage.

THE NEXT LEVEL
OF RELAXATION

Hard work pays off in the future. Ease pays off now.
—Source unknown

While most people believe they are not doing enough, their real problem is that they are too hard on themselves. In our culture, stress, overly high personal expectations, and nagging self-criticism put unnatural and debilitating pressure on us from within. The greatest gift you can give yourself, your wealth, and your life is to lighten up.

I work with a client who is highly successful but highly stressed. Sherry has built a prestigious company and sincerely seeks to serve her employees and her customers. But she assumes a tremendous burden that has yielded her significant physical and emotional pain. During a coaching session, Sherry told me that she has generated an "insane" upcoming travel schedule that moved her staff to urge her to take an assistant to lighten her load. Sherry declined the offer, citing that "I would not wish such a trip on anyone I loved." I pointed out to Sherry that while she was being kind to those she wished to spare from such duress, she did wish such a trip on someone she loved—herself. Why, I asked her, would you do to yourself what you would not do to someone else? Ultimately, she accepted an assistant for the trip and gave herself the precious gift of self-care.

While it is helpful to have goals just beyond your current reach and to strive to achieve them, if you use the process as an excuse to beat yourself up, you sabotage your success and undermine the joy of your journey. When I work with stressed overachievers, the client and I can usually trace the client's unreasonable self-demands back to a punitive parent or authority figure. No one is born with a critical voice in their head. All criticism is learned from other people who are hypercritical of themselves, and do not know how to alleviate their pain except by projecting it onto others. That is why *the critical voice is not your own.* Neither is the voice that pushes you to keep going and performing to a point that you reduce your life to a mere trickle.

If you tend to push yourself too hard, you are not likely going to stop overnight. Ingrained habits often take a while to undo themselves. If you apply a high-achievement ethic to your goal of relaxation, you will sabotage it. Your inner critic will demand that you *relax right now,* and do it perfectly and completely, otherwise you are a stupid failure—just another verse in an old sad song. (As the office sign warns, "The beatings will continue until morale improves.")

So how does a longtime overachiever reverse a trend and reclaim joy and satisfaction in his life?

First, recognize that what you have been doing has not brought you the happiness you seek. Money, maybe. Prestige and power, perhaps. Accolades, probably. Peace, no. If you have lost your inner peace, the money, prestige, power, and accolades don't mean diddly-squat. At some point nearly every obsessive overachiever realizes, there must be more to life than this. That is a very significant, even holy, point: you are ready and open to receive help.

Next, begin to notice when your compulsive overdoing starts not feeling good. You may experience physical symptoms such as headaches, digestive or eliminative issues, or heart or respiratory difficulties. Or you may become irritable, argumentative, or depressed. Or you may get some two-by-fours ("In-your-face productions") from the universe, such as a partner leaving you, getting fired, or legal trouble. Reframe all of these as wake-up calls. A loving, benevolent universe is advising you that you have taken a detour from happiness, and it is trying to show you the way home. At such a point, don't curse life—thank it.

Next, note that *there is always a next level of relaxation.* At the moment you recognize you are stressed, ask yourself what that next level is. You may not be able to go from point A to point Z in an instant, but you can go from point A to point B. That may be all you can do—but it may be all you need to do. Then, a while later, go from B to C, and so on.

Here are some examples of next levels you might seek:

- Take several long, slow deep breaths.
- Get up from your desk, go to the restroom, and splash some cold water on your face.
- Take a short walk.
- If you are in the midst of a heated argument, suggest a brief time-out for you to collect yourself.
- Phone a friend for a short chat.
- Head for the fitness center to work out.
- Get a massage.
- Put on your favorite music.
- Take a nap.
- Pray or meditate.
- Watch a fun movie.
- Play with the dog or cat.

These are just a few examples; do whatever works for you. Simply ask yourself what would bring a bit of relief here. Take the edge off your upset and you will see more clearly your next step—and maybe even save your health, marriage, or life.

I know an overworked fellow who owned a large hardware company. His personal coach suggested that he go to the office four days a week instead of five. (If five days a week sound like a small amount, this chapter is for you.) The fellow took his coach's advice, and used the extra day for personal renewal. He walked on the beach with his dog, read novels, and visited his grandkids. He reported to his coach that on that one extra day off he gained so much refreshment and insight that he became far more productive in his other four workdays than he had been in five. Eventually the company profits told the same story.

Small steps are good—they add up to big ones. Small steps are especially helpful to overachievers, who need to learn that life is less about getting somewhere, and more about being somewhere.

1. Do you push yourself too hard?

   Are you more demanding of yourself than others?

2. What critical or unkind statements do you make to yourself?

   Whose voice are those statements echoing?

3. What do you demand of yourself that you would not demand of someone you loved?

4. What physical, emotional, or situational symptoms tip you off that have gotten stressed?

5. Think of a situation about which you feel troubled or stressed.

   What is the next level of relaxation you could go to regarding this situation?

   If any other stressful situations come to mind, what would be your next level of relaxation for each of them?

AFFIRM:

> *I offer myself the kindness I would offer to one I loved.*
> *I reach for my next level of relaxation and let it help me.*

IF IT'S NOT FUN,
HIRE IT DONE

To find our calling is to find the intersection between
our own deep gladness and the world's deep hunger.
                                                    —Frederick Buechner

There are two groups of people whose lives and prosperity would change immensely if they let other people help them: creative artists and control freaks. I can't count the number of coaching conversations I have had that went something like this:

Client: *I love doing my art, but I don't know how to sell it.*
Me: *Get someone to help you.*
Client: *But I can't afford to hire someone.*
Me: *Find someone who understands and appreciates you and your work and offer them a percentage of the income they help you generate.*
Client: (Sits with a stunned look, like a deer in the headlights.) *Oh, yeah, cool . . . I hate doing that kind of stuff.*
Me: *You're not supposed to.*

Or:

Client: *I feel so stressed. My business is taking off and it demands nearly all my time. My wife is frustrated and angry at me, and I wish I had more time to spend with my kids.*

Me: *Hire someone to help you.*
Client: *But no one knows how to do what I do, and I don't think anyone can do it as well as me.*
Me: *Get over it. There are people who can do what you don't want to do, a lot better than you.*
Client: *So how do I find someone?*
Me: *Make a list of all the things you do not want to do. That becomes their job description.*
Client: *And then what do I do?*
Me: *Only what you love.*
Client: *That sounds too good to be true.*
Me: *It's actually good enough to be true.*

There are two types of people in the world: visionaries and executives. Visionaries have big ideas but don't want to be bothered with the details of carrying them out. Executives just love to get things done. It is rare that both trails coexist within one person. For that reason, we need each other. A partnership between a visionary and an executive is extremely powerful, and will yield both partners success and joy far beyond what they would reap if they each tried to do it all by themselves.

The answer to your business and prosperity questions is more simple than you have been told:

Be what you are and let life help you with what you are not.

If you hire the right person to help you and they do their job well, they will increase your income to pay your salary and theirs, and increase both. Then everyone wins.

Take Bill Gates, for example, the richest man in America. (You can track Bill's increasing wealth on several Web sites—some people have nothing better to do than count his money.) At Bill's current rate of income, if he was walking down a hall at Microsoft and he saw a thousand-dollar bill on the floor and bent over to pick it up, he would be making less money than if he did not stop at all. He is making more money during that time frame simply doing what he is doing. Mr. Gates is true to his role as a visionary and creator, and he has thousands of people executing his visions—many of whom love doing just that. Bill doesn't answer the reception phone or pick up copy machine paper from Staples or stock the Coke machine. He helps other people make money doing those tasks, and they help him make money doing what he does best. A winning formula, to be sure.

The most debilitating belief I encounter is that work requires suffering. The most liberating belief I encounter is that an authentic career is founded in joy. If this sounds alien to you, remember the words of the Wright brothers, who described their process of inventing the airplane thus: "We couldn't wait to get up in the morning." Behold the most telling feature of right livelihood. You, too, can enjoy such a blessed career, provided you are true to your unique gifts. Keep it simple: do what you love and let others do the rest. Then you will remember how good it can get, and live it.

Despair says I cannot lift that weight.
Happiness says I do not have to.

—James Richardson

1. What aspects of your work do you love?

2. What aspects of your work would you rather not do?

3. What would be the job description of the person you would bring aboard to do the things you would rather not do or are not skilled to do?

4. Do you believe that no one else can do everything you do as well as you?

   Are you open to considering the possibility that someone could do elements of your work with equal or greater skill?

5. How much would it be worth to you to have more free time and peace of mind?

AFFIRM:

I am true to my talents and joys,
and I let life help me with all else.

ROOM AT THE TOP
FOR EVERYONE

Give yourself abundant pleasure,
and you will have abundant pleasure to give to others.
—Neale Donald Walsch

While I was presenting a weekend seminar in Greece, a kindly man named George invited me to have lunch with him the following day, and I accepted. When the time came, however, I found myself not wanting to go. All I could think about was going back to my hotel room and resting. I apologetically told George that I needed some time off. To assuage my discomfort about changing our plans, I suggested that we sit together that evening at the nightclub gala banquet for seminar participants. George accepted the news and invitation graciously, and I looked forward to connecting with him that evening.

When the banquet began, however, I saw no sign of George. The gala went on, and George did not show up. Later on in the evening I noticed George in a booth toward the rear of the club, sitting cozily next to an attractive woman. The two were holding hands, talking, laughing, and obviously having a grand time.

"So there you are!" I greeted George. "I was wondering what happened to you."

"The most wonderful thing happened!" he replied, glowing. "When you and I didn't go out for lunch, I went with a small group and met Lena here." Lena put her arm on George's shoulder and smiled.

"We really like each other and we are enjoying getting to know each other."

I shook my head in amazement at the divine scheme of things. While I had felt guilty about canceling my lunch appointment with George, my choice was utterly in harmony with his best interests. Perhaps I paved the way for him to meet his mate!

There is no private good. What is truly right for you must ultimately serve others. You have likely been taught that it is selfish to ask for what you want; yet true self-care enhances your ability to care for others. *The universe operates on a win-win basis.* What works for you must, in the long run, work for others. Success is not competitive; it is multiplicative. There is room at the top for everyone.

When you are in your right place at the right time with the right people for the right purpose, you set the stage for others to do the same. If you hold yourself back because of fear, guilt, or feelings of obligation, you impede the flow of well-being and success. Your authenticity is the most direct route to achieve your goals and to help others achieve theirs. Strike the keynote of your joy, and you will create the optimal environment for your friends, family, clients, and even people you casually meet to do the same.

One evening, Dee and I went to a restaurant where we were seated under an air-conditioning unit. Dee felt chilly, and although we had already been served our appetizers, we asked the waiter if we could be reseated. We did not want to make extra work for the waiter, but we decided to trust the "no private good" principle. The waiter acceded to our request, and a few minutes later an elderly couple was seated at the table we had vacated. As soon as the couple sat down, the man breathed a sigh of relief and exclaimed, "Ah! Air-conditioning—just what I needed!"

Our good was intrinsically connected with the good of those patrons. If we had stayed where we were not happy because we felt too awkward to ask for our true choice, we might have thwarted the opportunity for that couple to receive the relief they sought. When we relaxed and trusted the big picture process, the door was opened for all of us to have everything we wanted.

Each of us must answer for himself a fundamental prosperity question:

Do we live in a universe of fixed and limited resources, or do we live in a universe of unlimited resources and possibilities, capable of fulfilling everyone's needs?

Meditate on this question and hold all of your choices up to it. You may be surprised to discover how many of your decisions affirm that there is not enough to go around. Such choices are usually based on fear. When you act out of fear you underscore it, and things do not get better, but worse.

By contrast, notice how you feel and the results you obtain when you choose from a vision of unlimited good. It is from this consciousness that all progress proceeds and miracles happen. Anwar Sadat declared: "You are not a realist unless you believe in miracles." It is also said, "Only those who see the invisible can do the impossible." When you shift your vision, you shift your results. When you change the way you see the world, the world you see will change.

There is enough of everything for everyone. Live as if you deserve all your heart's desires, and you will not only receive what you request but also pave the way for others to have their hearts' desires.

1. Is there something you want that you feel selfish about?

   How might your taking this action or obtaining this thing help others?

2. Is there something you want to say no to but feel guilty about?

   What might be the yes behind the no? What gift are you giving yourself or the other person by saying no?

3. Has someone said no to you recently, about which you feel hurt or rejected?

4. How might their no be a yes to something better for you?

AFFIRM:

The truer I am to myself, the more I help others.

FIVE: YOUR ECONOMY DEPENDS ON YOU

Generate, replicate, celebrate.

AN AUDIENCE
OF THOUSANDS

We need to learn to set our course by the stars,
not by the lights of every passing ship.

—Omar Nelson Bradley

I looked out over the seminar audience and felt disappointed that more people hadn't shown up. We had hoped for a hundred participants, but there sat only a dozen. As I tried to figure out why our attendance was so low, my emotions spiraled into a tailspin. Had the organizers not done enough promotion? Was the ticket price too high? Was I not a good enough presenter to attract a larger crowd? I felt embarrassed and didn't want to be there. The more I wallowed in disappointment, the more constricted I felt.

The program began with a musical presentation by a couple I met backstage. They seemed pleasant and upbeat. I took a seat among the meager crowd and waited for the opening act. Suddenly, the couple dashed onstage with explosive energy and enthusiasm. They bounded into their first song with a wave of joy and celebration that seemed far out of proportion to the number of people sitting before them. Within moments, everyone was clapping and singing along, then standing. Quickly, my energy lifted and I was glad to be there. The duo performed several more dynamic selections and established the tone for what turned out to be a powerful evening. Although these musicians were performing for but a few, they gave of themselves as if they were playing for a packed house in Las Vegas, and set the stage for a successful event.

I learned a huge lesson that night: as a performer, salesperson, manager, parent, teacher, counselor, healer, or professional of any kind, you must be *self-igniting*. You cannot afford to base your performance on the situation you step into. If you let external conditions determine your attitude, your success will be conditional. If you let your vision establish your attitude, your success will be unconditional. Your intention and energy must be so strong that you *create* conditions rather than react to them.

When your actions or happiness depend on external factors, you will bob up and down like a cork on the surface of a turbulent ocean. Your days and career will be an emotional roller coaster. You will feel stressed and frazzled, and your journey may be compounded with relationship conflicts and health problems. When you give your power away to people and circumstances, which are fickle and transitory, your life will be out of control.

If, on the other hand, you source your experience from your inner spirit, you call forth your power to generate dynamic results and enjoy the process. Then you are the master of your career, destiny, and life. Your energy proceeds from your choices, not the marketplace.

Resolve now to set your own tone, no matter what appearances may indicate. Be bigger than your circumstances, and your circumstances will reform themselves to reflect your intentions. You do not have to sweat and struggle to create a positive shift in your audience, clients, or students. Most people attempt to generate success by manipulating people and things around them. They do not realize that the first step to real change is to shift yourself. When you are established in a higher consciousness, conditions will align with your elevated thoughts, with far less effort on your part than if you tried to fix people and things. As James Allen wrote, "We think in secret, and it comes to pass; environment is our looking glass."

Those who soar beyond the masses or appearances are not bound by time, season, or personal limits. Mel Tormé wrote his classic *Christmas Song* ("Chestnuts roasting on an open fire . . .") during the month of June. Oscar Hammerstein composed his most beloved musical, *The Sound of Music,* while he was dying. Franklin Delano Roosevelt guided America through a world war while he was confined to a wheelchair. Greatness knows not the limits from which fear would shy away.

In the aftermath of the terrorism of September 11, 2001, most people feared to fly and the travel industry plunged into deep dregs. Many travel businesses went belly-up. Around March 2002, I read a newspaper article highlighting a small group of travel agents who were thriving. These businesses had scheduled vacation packages for the spring of 2002, even during the fall of 2001. While many other agents became immobilized during the doldrums following September 11, a few recognized that at some point people would feel ready and desirous to travel again. When spring came, these agents had their tours in place and were happy and able to accommodate customers. Their higher vision prevailed over current appearances.

Mentally go to your goal before your body begins. A basketball star was asked how he achieved such a high scoring percentage. "The ball is in the basket before it leaves my hand," he answered. The Bible teaches: "Give thanks for the answer to your prayer before you see it." Instead of moving *toward* your goal, live *from* it, and you will achieve extraordinary results. There is a place in consciousness where your dream has already come true. Visit it frequently, and it will not be long before you live it in your daily life.

It's easy and natural to feel enthusiastic when business and income are showing up and things are going your way. But those who can generate enthusiasm when indicators are down are true masters. The tide rises and falls, but your sense of well-being proceeds from a source far deeper and stronger than worldly fortune. Tap into it, and you become the ruler of your destiny.

1. What people or things do you allow to determine your energy or happiness?

How do you give your power away to them?

Think of a time when you did not let others determine your mood or reaction. What did you know and feel in that moment that allowed you to rise beyond conditions?

2. Who is the most self-generating person you know?

What does this person do that makes him or her successful?

3. Choose a specific goal you would like to achieve.

This week, take ten minutes each day to fantasize about how it would feel if you had already manifested it. Close your eyes and get into the feeling of your intention, until it seems real. Then watch what happens.

AFFIRM:

I am the creator of my experience.
I establish my vision in joy, success, and service,
and my life reflects my intentions.

A PERSONAL
ECONOMY

A visionary thrives under all conditions.

—Abraham-Hicks

The Great Depression was a hard time for many people, but not for all. During those years while many were struggling, some were prospering and accomplishing extraordinary achievements.

It was during the Depression that the greatest architectural feats of the twentieth century were achieved. The Empire State Building, which has graced the Manhattan skyline and inspired countless New Yorkers, tourists, and lovers, was erected during America's leanest years. The cornerstone of the building was laid in 1931 and rose to become the world's tallest building at an unprecedented rate of 4.5 stories per week, completed in only fourteen months. The final cost was $41 million (equivalent to $603 million today), advanced by private financiers.

Across the country another technological marvel was unfolding. The Golden Gate Bridge, long eschewed as a pipedream, was approved by Bay Area voters in 1930 by way of a $35 million bond (or $500 million today). The bridge required the tallest towers, the longest, thickest cables, and the largest underwater foundation piers ever built, posted beneath a sea believed by many to be impossibly turbulent. Yet 1937 brought the opening of the bridge, which to this day stands as a symbol of the triumph of intention. While many in the country were

focusing their attention on what they were missing, others were investing their vision, faith, and dollars in what could be.

No matter what the predominant economic trend, some people
struggle and others thrive. The difference has little to do with external
conditions, and a lot to do with personal consciousness. Many investors' joy rises and falls with the stock market. Deliberate creators, on
the other hand, recognize that their prosperity depends not on what
happens outside them, but what they generate *inside* them. They understand their power to alter their experience by choosing the thoughts
they would dwell on. Thus they generate abundance in accord with
their expansive vision.

I worked at a store owned by a man who was prone to complaints
and excuses. As his business lost more and more money, he blamed
every possible condition outside himself: the economy, the weather, his
employees, inept suppliers, and anything else he could think of.
Eventually his store went out of business, for a long list of reasons he
could recite if asked.

Just two miles away there was a similar store, and it was thriving.
This store was subject to the same conditions my boss complained
about, yet it was succeeding financially. The crucial difference between
the two stores was the attitude of the managers. The other store manager was upbeat, she loved what she did, made customer service a high
priority, and took responsibility for following through on the tasks my
boss blamed others for not doing. It was no accident that my employer's store failed while the other one hummed.

While the two stores were a short physical distance apart, the two
owners lived in drastically different economies, which had nothing to
do with how much money was flowing through the nation; they had
more to do with the thoughts and attitudes flowing through the psy-
ches of the proprietors.

The conditions that other people draw unto them need not affect
you in the same way. If a doctor cites you statistics of how long you

will take to heal or how long you will live as per your current diagnosis; or a reading-glasses display tells what strength prescription you need according to your age; or a psychologist tells you the chances of your new marriage succeeding based on your number of previous marriages—these advisers are making their assumptions on the basis of the statistics of what has happened to others who have gone before you in similar situations. The one factor they cannot calculate is your unique consciousness. Just because others have run their energy in a certain way does not mean you have to or will run your energy in a like manner. If you make different mental, emotional, or attitudinal choices, you will create different results.

When I toured the Soviet Union years ago, I visited a church in a small town where the townspeople have traditionally venerated an icon of the Virgin Mary. During a plague that ran rampant in all the surrounding areas and proved fatal for most, no one in the town was touched by it. Such is the power of faith and focused consciousness.

You have the power to thrive under all conditions. You have the power to live by choice. You are as prosperous as you think. You are doing better than you think you are, and you have more opportunities than you know. Remind yourself of the well-being available to you, and even while others may settle for little, you will build sparkling towers and span bridges across churning seas.

Those who say it can't be done
are usually interrupted by others doing it.

—James Baldwin

1. Have you ever succeeded at a project when others were failing at something similar, or you were told that you had little chance to succeed?

What was the difference between your attitude and theirs?

2. Does the economy determine attitude, or does attitude determine economy?

Which variable is a more powerful influence?

Which variable do you have the most control over?

3. To what external conditions have you given your power away (for example, the stock market, weather, news, month's receipts, job market, other people's attitudes)?

Practice paying no attention to these variables; determine to be happy and positive no matter what is happening around you or other people are saying and doing.

AFFIRM:

My economy depends on me.
I source desirable conditions and results.

NOT ENOUGH
HEADSTANDS

Better to write for yourself and have no public,
than to write for the public and have no self.

—Cyril Connolly

A fter mailing out a newsletter including an article about a contro-versial subject, I received several letters of complaint from people whose opinions differed from mine. They did not like my humor and took offense at some of my comments. I felt disturbed by this feedback, since I meant no harm and I sincerely desired to empower my readers, not insult them.

At a seminar soon afterward, I recounted the situation to the par-ticipants, who offered me some helpful responses. One fellow asked me, "How many newsletters did you send out?"

"About three thousand."

"And how many letters of complaint did you receive?"

"About three."

"Well, that's a pretty good batting average!" he noted.

The most poignant insight came from a fellow named Scott. "You know, Alan," Scott told me, "two of the things I most appreciate about you are your sense of humor and your ability to take lightly issues that other people take seriously. If you stop joking, *I* will be disappointed and offended . . . *then* what will you do?"

Scott's comments put the situation in perspective. I realized that no matter what I do, some people will agree and like me, and others won't. I could not do enough headstands to keep everyone around me happy all the time. My job is not to try to be everything to everyone, but to be who and what I am. When popularity becomes more important than authenticity, you compromise yourself and sacrifice your happiness. When I came to this realization, I let go of my self-doubt with a welcome sigh of relief and felt a great weight lift off my shoulder.

If you try to build your life around the expectations of others, you are doomed to frustration. At one of my Hawaii seminars one participant voiced many complaints: the retreat center was too rustic; her bed was too hard; the food did not satisfy her diet; and on and on. My staff and I tried to satisfy her requests, but it seemed that no matter what we did, it was not enough. I was concerned that maybe we should revisit our site choice so we could please all the customers.

After our program this woman and another participant spent several days at a luxury resort on Maui. Afterward I asked her roommate how the two of them enjoyed the hotel. "I liked it just fine," the woman answered. "But my roommate complained the whole time. Nothing the hotel did for her could make her happy." Then I recognized it was not our center that was the problem; it was the dark glasses through which this participant viewed her life. So it is for all of us, for better or worse.

No one has ever succeeded in pleasing everyone, and you won't be the first. Even Jesus, Buddha, Gandhi, Martin Luther King Jr., the Dalai Lama, and many pure-hearted world change agents incurred the wrath of those who did not understand them. You can be absolutely correct, and some will scorn you. When Galileo asserted that the Earth was round, not flat, the Church considered his proposition heresy and sentenced him to life imprisonment. (To this day there is a society of "Flat Earth" believers who argue that all the photos of Earth taken from space are contrived and the moon program was a hoax.) Great world-movers do not turn back or compromise their integrity for the sake of popular opinion. They are true to the inner guidance and their relationship with their Higher Power. Rather than please people, they please their soul, which is all that really matters.

One of my clients was diagnosed with cancer, and after a few chemotherapy treatments she decided to take an alternative medicine route. "When I told my friends that I was doing chemotherapy, my holistic-minded friends freaked out," she explained. "And when I told my conventional-minded friends I was going for alternative medicine, they got really upset," she added. So what's a person to do? You have no choice but to go with your strongest inner guidance.

Tom Peters, author of *In Search of Excellence* and one of the most respected experts in business, states that "unless you are receiving negative feedback from twenty percent of your constituents, you probably aren't doing anything worthwhile." He also notes that after he presents a seminar on passion and integrity in business, "unless some of your employees quit, we are doing something wrong." So disagreement, adversity, or shake-ups within an organization may not be a sign that things are falling apart; they may indicate that things are coming together.

While you don't want to purposely offend anyone, you can't afford to take it personally if someone disagrees with you or gets upset over your actions. If after prayer, consideration, and introspection you believe that your intentions are pure and you are in integrity with your values, mentally and emotionally release your critic and, as we are told in the Bible, "Shake the dust off your feet, and move on."

1. Over the course of your life, who have you tried to please the most?

How did your attempts to please others cost you your own integrity or inner peace?

What did you learn from trying to get others to maintain a high opinion of you?

2. Is there anyone in your life now whom you are trying to please at the expense of your joy?

How could you upgrade your thoughts and actions to keep your peace?

3. Is there anything you would like to do, but are not doing because you fear negative opinion?

How might you reframe your vision of this goal to inspire you to do it?

AFFIRM:
I live true to my own path and I allow others the same freedom.
I am motivated by inner knowing rather than public opinion.

WHO'S WORKING
FOR WHOM?

A man of good will with a little effort and belief in his own pow-
ers can enjoy a deep, tranquil, rich life—provided he go his
own way.

—Henry Miller

While negotiating to buy a parcel of real estate, I discovered some information about the property that lessened its value. In light of the deficiency, I told my real estate agent to reduce my offer by $25,000. My agent, I discovered, was a sheepish negotiator. "I doubt if the seller will go for that," she replied meekly.

I felt that I needed to make a stand. "I need you to go to bat for me. Please align with my intentions here."

"All right, all right," she answered apologetically. "If that is what you want to offer, I will present it."

She telephoned me a few minutes later. "I have good news: the seller accepted your offer."

The interest on the $25,000 I saved in the negotiation equaled another $25,000 over the term of the loan. So that one piece of negotiation represented a savings of $50,000. I was certainly glad I asked my agent to step up to the plate and represent my intentions fully.

When you hire a professional, that person is your agent and you are paying them to help you accomplish your chosen goals. Doctors, lawyers, therapists, architects, talent agents, and decorators are there to assist you in manifesting your vision, not the one they would choose for you. When working with an agent of any kind, be sure your visions are aligned.

A friend informed me that she had hired a certain fellow to manage her popular gift shop, which was respected as customer friendly. The new manager, however, had a reputation as a hard-nosed, abrasive, in-your-face salesman. I told the owner why I thought this fellow might not be her best choice. My friend became defensive and told me she was determined to follow through. Several months later, she phoned me and told me that she had fired the manager after he had alienated a number of customers, and she could not have a manager treating her clients less kindly than she herself would treat them.

Your choice of a doctor or medical professional is equally important. If you are working with someone to create health and well-being, be sure that person holds a similar vision. Many doctors, well-meaning and skilled though they are, are trained to pay more attention to what is deficient and hold you in an identity of illness than to pursue what is efficient and hold you in an identity of wholeness. Do you feel better or worse after you spend time with your doctor or practitioner? The better you feel about the person you are working with, the more likely you are to achieve the results you seek.

When my neighbor's dog was seriously injured, she took him to a veterinarian who gave the pet a dire prognosis. The dog tried to rally, but experienced complications, and every time his owner took him to the vet, the doctor found another problem. After a while, my neighbor grew frustrated with the dog's continued illness and she took him to another vet. The moment this doctor entered the exam room, my neighbor felt relieved. He smiled and assured her that the dog would be well soon, and he put the dog on a far simpler regime than the original vet. The dog was up and about quickly, to the great delight of his owner.

Another friend was seeking to create an amicable divorce. Her lawyer was pushing her to attack and destroy, a tactic that did not represent the kind of energy or results the client was seeking to create. I counseled her to advise her attorney to represent her intentions, for she was the one who would have to live with the results. My friend and her lawyer ultimately took a gentler course and eventually created a win-win relationship with her ex-husband, which bore positive effects on their children.

Certainly a good professional can and should advise and make suggestions based on their expertise. Be open to hear, respect, and weigh your agent's advice. Try it on for size, sleep on it, pray about it, and be with it. If you can stand behind it with confidence and enthusiasm, move with it. A good agent can often do a better job for you than you would do for yourself. If, however, after deliberation and introspection, you would not choose to move in a particular direction, you cannot afford to do so. Be clear with your agent about your desired goals. A good agent will respect your intentions and do their best to carry them out. It could be worth $50,000 to ask for what you want. It could be worth a lot more: your peace of mind and the deep satisfaction of knowing that you have acted in accord with your real values and choices.

1. Name an agent you have worked with who represented your intentions and helped you achieve what you wanted.

Name another agent who did not represent your intentions.

What lessons did you learn from these experiences?

2. Consider an agent with whom you are currently working.

On a scale of 1–10, how well is your agent representing your interests?

In what areas is your agent representing you well?

What areas would you like to bolster or improve?

What could you say or do to upgrade your agent's representation?

3. If you are an agent serving others, how might you better attune to their needs so you represent them even better?

AFFIRM:

I attract professionals aligned with my purpose.
My agents represent my intentions,
and together we achieve the highest goals.

SIX: CIRCULATE, CIRCULATE, CIRCULATE

Moving wealth out

moves wealth in.

MANY AVENUES

My will shall shape my future.
Whether I fail or succeed shall be no man's doing but my own.
I am the force;
I can clear any obstacle before me or I can be lost in the maze.
My choice, my responsibility;
win or lose, only I hold the key to my destiny.

—Elaine Maxwell

I received an invitation from a prestigious company to present a lecture to a vast audience at a large conference in a major city. I was elated! This significant exposure, accompanied by hefty book sales, represented a major career boost for me. I would most likely go on to join the roster of regular speakers at huge events this company produced half a dozen times a year in popular centers around the country. A momentous coup, to be sure!

A few days later, I received another letter from the company informing me they would regretfully have to rescind. They had hired me to replace another speaker they had intended to dismiss, but upon further research they realized they were still contractually obligated to her. After all was said and done, she was in and I was out.

I felt crestfallen, frustrated, and teased. My big opportunity had slipped right through my fingers! How could this happen? I started to feel depressed.

At the time I received the news, I was visiting with a friend who heard my story and noticed my upset. She listened for a while and then asked me, "Might there be a gift in this?"

A gift? What gift could there possibly be? The whole situation seemed to be just a disappointing mess. I took a deep breath and thought about it for a while. Then an idea occurred to me that liberated me and changed my life.

I realized that this production company was not the sole source of my prosperity. It was but one avenue through which my good could flow. There were many more channels through which attractive opportunities and prosperity could come to me. I had ascribed undue power to this company. It was my friend—not my savior.

The true source of my abundance, I recognized, is not a person or an organization, but life itself. When I understood this, I was free. My pain, frustration, and distress lifted, and I felt even more empowered than when I had anticipated speaking.

Since that day I have not identified any one person or company as the source of my good. Anyone or anything can bring me prosperity. And my career has not suffered in the least. I have gone on to receive expanding income through many different channels.

A fascinating postscript: a few years later the same company offered me an attractive publishing contract. Ultimately, we created an association that has proved very rewarding for both of us.

We tend to identify individuals or institutions as the source of our empowerment, when they are simply venues for a universal source. An ancient eastern metaphor suggests that when you see rainwater pouring out of the mouth of a cement gargoyle adorning the roof of a classical building, it would appear that the water is coming from the gargoyle. In truth, the water is issuing from the infinite sky; the gargoyle just catches the water and funnels it.

When you are ripe and ready for a right relationship, car, home, job, physical healing, or any desired next step, there are thousands of ways your riches can come to you. If you fixate on one of those avenues and demand that your success arrive through it alone, you set yourself up for frustration, pain, and conflict, and delay or cut off the many other ways the universe can provide for you.

"If you can't pray a door open, don't try to pry it open." From the level of the human personality or ego, you cannot know enough variables about a situation to play God and make it happen in a certain way. Perhaps there are reasons one way isn't working and another is. It may simply be a matter of timing. Can you trust that life may have a better idea for you?

Rather than dictating the size, shape, and color of the package you seek, focus on its essence. Pray or hold an intention for your desired *qualities* of the position or relationship. Ask, for example, for a position that is stimulating, financially rewarding, and passionate for you, with coworkers you enjoy and a mission you resonate with. Then let universal wisdom put a name, location, and details on the answer to your prayer. You may find that divine intelligence is far more resourceful than you know, and things are working out in your favor even—sometimes especially—when you do not see how.

1. Do you feel dependent on a particular company as the source of your financial well-being?

   Does this relationship generate any anxiety for you?

   How might your supply of good come to you in other ways?

2. Do you feel dependent on a particular person as the source of your love?

   Does this relationship generate any anxiety for you?

   How might your supply of love come to you in other ways?

3. Read Psalm 23 and meditate on each verse until you feel safe and secure at the center of your being.

AFFIRM:

My good finds me through many different avenues.
I release any person or company as the source of my prosperity.
I gratefully allow the universe to provide for me
in clever and wondrous ways.

HAPPY MONEY

If there is to be any peace,
it will come through being, not having.

—Henry Miller

At the conclusion of a seminar I presented, the sponsor sat down with me to settle the finances. After recapping the figures, she added, "Two people came to me at intermission and told me they did not like the program. So I gave them a refund. I hope it's okay with you. I want to receive only happy money."

Of course it was all right with me. I, too, value "happy money." Happy money is income received from someone who gives it willingly, with appreciation for the goods or service rendered. It represents a positive exchange and satisfaction by all parties.

When you fight over money, force someone to pay who does not want to pay, or do not refund money requested, you get to keep the money—but you also get to keep the dark energy surrounding the interaction. Someone out there is angry with you and will probably say unkind things about you and your business. The interaction will linger in a negative emotional space, certainly for the customer and probably for you. Is it really worth it?

I stayed at a hotel that offers a full satisfaction guarantee. If, as a guest, you do not enjoy your stay for any reason, the hotel will not charge you for your visit. I asked a hotel executive how many people take them up on this offer. "Fewer than one percent," she answered. I am certain that in the long run the hotel is generating far more income through their commitment to service than they are losing on their low number of refunds.

The principle of happy money can be applied to relationships, as well. I know a woman who divorced a multimillionaire and asked him for nothing when she left. She would have been entitled to quite a sum if she sued. "I just wanted to end my marriage, and I didn't want anything gluing us together. If I sued him and he had to pay me alimony, perhaps with resentment, over a long period of time, that would have kept me in a relationship with him in ways that were very distasteful to me. I am very happy now, and glad to get on with my life. I don't want that marriage, and I don't want his money." She later entered another marriage in which she and her husband prospered immensely. So she lost nothing in the process.

Apply the *happy money* principle to money you spend, as well. If you are not happy about paying for something, explain to the vendor why, and tell them what you are willing to pay for and what you are not. In most cases, you can reach a happy medium that leaves both parties satisfied. If not, just make your best effort and keep checking in with your sense of integrity. If you are right with yourself, you are right with the universe.

Does the happy money principle mean that you just give everyone everything they want, even if their request is unjustified? No, there are cases in which integrity calls for you to say no or to ask for what you deserve. Hold the interaction in a calm and sensible light and speak your truth. Go not to drama, but reason, and trust that honesty is powerful. Do not use the interaction as an excuse for upset, but see it as an opportunity to connect. Keep spirit first and the money will take care of itself.

If you find yourself in a situation in which you must pay but would rather not, reframe your experience to remember that the abundant universe can always provide for you, and the money will likely return through another door. Your attitude about money is far more significant than any one transaction, and your wealth is far vaster.

Happy money is a rewarding guiding principle in the course of business and friendship. It will turn business *into* friendship. When in doubt, give. By the same token, let the universe give to you through ingenious and creative means. Rise beyond resentment as both a receiver and payer. Then the life force energy we call money becomes the blessing it was meant to be.

1. Are you trying to squeeze money out of someone who is unwilling to pay?

> What is the emotional, energetic, or financial cost of hassling them?

> For a moment, try on for size the thought of just letting the issue go. How does this feel?

2. Are you paying for anything with resentment?

> What would it take for you to change the situation so it is resentment-free?

3. If you knew you had access to an infinite supply of money, love, and well-being, how would you be seeing and handling the above interactions differently?

4. How would your life and work change if you adopted a happy money policy?

AFFIRM:

> *I give and receive money with joy and appreciation.*
> *I trust universal supply to take care of me*
> *and everyone with whom I interact.*

WORK WITH
THE WILLING

Be an all-out, not a hold-out.

—Norman Vincent Peale

A motivational teacher scheduled a weeklong seminar for a small group, and had one space left. Two people applied for the opening, for which the tuition was $2,000. One of the applicants was a wealthy woman who tried to bargain with the seminar leader, offering him $1,500 for the tuition. The other applicant was a young man who had little money, but offered all he could—$500.

"Which student did you accept?" I asked the teacher.

"The young man," he replied.

"Why is that?" I asked.

"He gave everything," the teacher answered.

When you give or invest money or material things, the crucial factor is not how much you give; it is the energy and intent behind what you give. If you are holding back financially or energetically, the value of your investment is offset. In his illuminating book *You Can Have It All*, Arnold Patent explains that when we purposely withhold money, we are withholding love. We believe we can manipulate the other person by keeping something back from them, but in the long run we lose because whatever we withhold, we withhold from ourselves. The point of this teaching is not necessarily that you should give more money (which can be a great deal of fun); it is to encourage you to *be total* in whatever gifts or investments you make.

In the above story, the teacher was more interested in the student's investment of self than his investment of money. Someone who has a lot of money but gives little has less invested than one who has a little money but gives all. The teacher recognized that the student who showed up with a whole heart would receive more for himself and make a richer, energetic contribution to the group.

When you make it your intention to work with the willing, the quality of everything you do upgrades dramatically. Why play with someone who does not really want to be there? This principle applies to business relationships, romance, and friendships. How difficult it is to get anything done with someone who is not really present or has a mixed agenda. And how powerful it is to play with people who are on the same team with the same vision!

The *work with the willing* principle applies to *your* presence, too. If you participate in a business, relationship, or project, be sure that you are fully willing. If you are half present, you detract from your experience and make it harder for others. *Either do it with a whole heart, or don't do it.* You will be amazed at how much more powerful your actions and results are when you are true to this intention.

I had an assistant whose commitment to the job was wishy-washy. Ben showed up late and found reasons to leave the office, and his work was mediocre. But I thought I would give him a chance to get into the groove.

After a while, Ben got involved in a network marketing business he was excited about—so much that he worked it during his paid hours at my office. He fielded calls on his cell phone with far more enthusiasm than he handled our business calls. Finally, I told Ben: "I see you have more passion for your network marketing than for our business. I want you to be where your passion lives. You deserve a job you love, and we deserve an assistant who really wants to be here." I meant it; I really wanted everyone to be in their right place. We had an amicable parting, which opened the door for a new assistant who really wanted to be there and did a far better job.

Because we are spiritual beings, it is the spirit of what we do that determines how much fulfillment we derive. You can be going through all the motions and doing all the appropriate and expected actions, but if you are empty or absent inside, your deeds mean little. Only soul satisfaction can fulfill you; everything else will leave you hungry. Spiritual teacher Paramahansa Yogananda noted: "Manners without sincerity are like a beautiful but dead woman." Essence is more important than appearance.

When evaluating what someone is offering or giving you, or what you are offering, appraise it by the investment of spirit rather than material. An inexpensive, personally crafted gift from the heart can mean much more than an expensive jewel. Ask any mother how much she appreciates the drawing her little child made for her, and she will tell you it is priceless. The real jewel of life is your presence. Deliver that, and you will enrich everyone you touch, beginning with yourself.

1. Are you now doing anything with less than a whole heart?

   Why is your spirit not fully present?

   What would it take for you to participate wholly?

2. Are you now working or relating with someone who is not fully present?

   Why do you think they are not there?

   What would it take for them to be there and how could you support them?

3. Consider the situations in #1 and #2 above and take a few minutes each day to visualize each of these situations with everyone involved making a total investment. In your imaging, do not try to force yourself or another person into an action. Instead, attune to the picture and feeling of the final result, and let the universe arrange the methods and the players.

AFFIRM:

I bring my full presence to all I do,
and I prosper with everyone I touch.

GIVE IT ALL

Some people never know how much they have
until they discover how much they can give.
                    —Tagline for the movie *Good Will Hunting*

Andrew knew he had come to the end of his rope when he found himself scrounging behind the cushions of his couch, hoping to find some coins so he could buy some lunch. Not long ago, he was a successful executive; now he was a million dollars in debt. "There must be some way out of this," he told himself as he gathered a few dollars and went out to get a sandwich.

On his way back from the deli, Andrew was confronted by a homeless man. The fellow looked hungry and asked Andrew for a handout. Andrew's first thought was, "Are you kidding? I'm on the verge of being homeless myself!"

But then Andrew heard another voice within him: "Give him all you have." This guidance felt so compelling that Andrew decided to override his fear. He reached into his pocket and gave the homeless man all the change he had left, leaving himself with no money at all.

Immediately, Andrew felt not poorer but richer. Something about giving everything opened a door that was closed when he lived in fear. He felt free, better than he had in a long time.

As he walked home, Andrew thought of a company he could approach for a job. He had worked in the stock market, and he figured this company might be able to use his services. He called the firm and got an interview. The manager decided to take a small risk on Andrew and offered him a thousand dollars to research and evaluate a small business the firm was considering investing in. Andrew was thrilled to have a shot at generating some income, and gladly accepted. He visited the company, a start-up based on ecological values, and decided it would be a worthy investment. He submitted his recommendation and his employer agreed to go with it.

Within a short time, the ecology company skyrocketed to one of the ten hot stocks on the market. Andrew's employer was elated, and asked him how much of a salary he wanted in exchange for managing the account on a permanent basis. The largest amount Andrew could utter without gagging was "$10,000 a month" (meanwhile expecting that if he got half that figure, he would be lucky). His bosses conferred and told him that $100,000 a year was the best they could do. "Well, I guess so," Andrew told them. He was back in the game.

The stock continued to go through the roof, and Andrew negotiated a bonus based on a percentage of the company's earnings from the investment. Within a year, he made his million dollars back.

Now Andrew is immensely prosperous. He owns several successful businesses and has homes in three states. His turning point, he affirms, was the moment he decided to give all he had.

When you put fear, self-pity, and poverty thoughts aside, you become a conduit for money, energy, and success. Suddenly, you have access to resources that were absent when you saw through a filter of limitation. When you focus on lack and smallness, you hamper your ability to see solutions. As you relax and trust in universal supply, you expand your vision to discover your next step to success.

Your actions demonstrate what you believe. If you want to know what you believe, observe how you are living and feeling. When you hoard or hold back from letting your resources flow, you attest that there is a limited amount available to you and you must protect yourself from loss. When you stay in the current of expressing and sharing your wealth—even if it appears to be small—you affirm there is enough for yourself and everyone. Then life can and will manifest your affirmation.

Master metaphysician Florence Scovel Shinn explained: "All sickness is due to congestion and all healing is due to circulation." This principle applies to prosperity as well. When your mind is congested with thoughts of lack, resistance, and struggle, money cannot come to you or through you. Prime the pump of your consciousness by giving freely, and the universe will give freely to you.

Giving 99 percent is hard, but giving 100 percent is easy. The more you give, the more you have to give.

1. Are you withholding giving (money or anything else) to anyone?

   To whom and why?

   How does withholding from them equate to withholding from yourself?

2. Who are you the most generous with?

   How does this feel and what kind of results do you experience?

3. Who is the most generous person you know?

   What have you learned from this person?

4. If you fully trusted in the circulation of abundance in the universe, what would you be doing differently with your money or resources?

AFFIRM:

   I open to give to others, and the universe opens to give to me.

PAID IN LOVE

Choose a job you love
and you will never work another day in your life.

—Confucius

The East Maui Animal Refuge is a sanctuary for injured, unwanted, and unloved creatures, a home to animals the Humane Society would otherwise put to sleep. Whenever I drive through the refuge's gate, I feel tears well up. A big, blind, black Lab nuzzles under my hand; a fuzzy little terrier in a makeshift wheelchair ambles by; a deer licks the bandage on its knee; a chorus of meows issues from the tree house for cats with feline AIDS; and a motley menagerie of four hundred birds, goats, pigs, cows, and other Old MacDonald critters somehow coexist peacefully. It is a holy place.

Directors Sylvan and Suzie Schwab have run their homespun operation entirely on donations since they founded the refuge in 1983. They work tirelessly and selflessly from dawn till dusk, spending most of their time feeding hungry mouths, bandaging wounds, and administering medication. Along the way, the Schwabs have attracted many dedicated volunteers. Theirs is truly a labor of love.

The first time I visited the refuge, Sylvan and I were walking through his office, where I observed a tall stack of bills on his desk. "How do you stay afloat?" I asked him.

He smiled. "We just pay what we can when we can. People understand what we are trying to do here."

"And how do you pay your staff?" I asked.

"Oh, nobody gets any money here. Everyone here gets paid in love," Sylvan explained.

Money is just one form of compensation for service. There are many ways the universe will thank and take care of you in appreciation for the gifts you share. Do not evaluate your compensation by dollars alone. You may be getting paid in ways far more precious than money.

Many people make vast amounts of money but suffer terrible psychological and emotional ills because they are disconnected from their spirit. *If all you are receiving for your work is money, you are being grossly underpaid.* Others make little or no money, but sleep well at night, with a heart fulfilled. While money and satisfaction are certainly not mutually exclusive, true reward goes far beyond money.

Consider the many ways you may be paid, or are paying others: working in a soul-nurturing environment; developing valuable skills; being in the presence of a respected mentor; learning priceless life lessons; discovering more about who you are; creating potential business contacts; growing meaningful personal relationships; bringing greater health and vitality to your physical body; discovering what is not for you, so you know better what you would choose; and many more.

Practicing the principles in this book can and will help you attract more money for the things you want. You deserve to have all the money you want and need for everything your heart desires; not just to pay your bills but also to have and do things you enjoy. Do not stop short of that. Along the way, however, remember that money is never the goal; it is a by-product of joy. Your real goal is soul satisfaction. If your spirit is at peace, you will attract everything you need. If your heart is not satisfied, nothing you attract will get you what you want.

I knew an uptight woman who struggled with many emotional, mental, physical, and financial problems. Then she took a volunteer position helping AIDS babies. Once a week she went to a hospital and just held and cuddled these children. Quickly, her life was trans-

formed and her problems dissipated. She moved from a dollar economy to a love economy.

Spirit is the strongest (and only real) currency. Keep the current of
spirit flowing throughout your day, and your needs will be met. Don't
just make a living; make a life. Universal prosperity principles are simple, consistent, and always within your ability to use for your benefit
and that of others. Keep seeking a job that pays in love, and pay others in that currency, and you will never go hungry. And the money will
come. The money will come.

After a magazine reporter interviewed Sylvan Schwab about his life
at the East Maui Animal Refuge, she concluded that the man was
something of a saint. She told him, "I'm sure you are one person who
will go to heaven."

"Go to heaven?" Sylvan reflected. "I'm already there."

1. Are you doing anything now for money alone?

   How does it feel?

2. Describe a job you had (or have) in which your compensation went beyond money.

   What did you receive that you did not get in jobs based solely on financial gain?

3. Have you ever done something for joy alone, and money followed?

4. If you were to create a career based on joy and inner fulfillment, what would that be?

   Describe what you would be doing and how it would feel.

AFFIRM:

The universe pays me to live from my heart.
I give and receive love generously,
and money comes in the right way and time.

OUT OF THE
EQUATION

You should be thinking about the omelet,
not the price of the omelet.

—Embassy Suites advertisement

I opened the letter and read the invitation: *You have been selected to be a keynote speaker for our conference in Hawaii.* "Yes!" I shouted out loud—a free trip to paradise! Then I read the second page: *The policy of our conference is that presenters do not receive an honorarium. They also pay their own airfare, lodging, meals, and a conference registration fee.*

Well, *that won't quite do,* I grumbled to myself. *People pay me well to do this, including all my expenses!* Indignant, I tossed the letter into the wastebasket and paced around my living room.

I felt disappointed. I really wanted to go to Hawaii. Unsettled, I decided to sit down and meditate to clear my mind and calm my emotions. After a few minutes I relaxed and experienced a vision: I saw the face of an old leathery-skinned yogi with a turban, long white beard, and twinkling eyes. The yogi seemed to be hovering in front of me, smiling gently as if he were blessing me. Before long I forgot about my upset and sank into a blissful peace.

When I arose from the meditation, I felt much better. The idea of going to Hawaii continued to call me. Then I remembered a teaching I had heard: When confused about a decision, take money out of the equation.

What would I do if money were not an issue? Well, that was a no-brainer. For sure I would go. That settled it. On sheer intuition I retrieved the letter from the trash and inked my consent.

The next evening a friend invited me to attend a program she was hosting at her home. I didn't know the subject of the program, but something inside me said *go*. So I drove an hour through a cold New Jersey winter night to attend. Upon my arrival I met the presenter, who, I learned, had come to speak about the very Hawaii conference to which I had been invited. Bingo! When the third slide flashed on the screen, my jaw dropped nearly to the floor—it was a photo of the yogi I had seen in my meditation. "This is Sant Kirpal Singh," the speaker announced, "the founder of the Human Unity Conference." I needed no further signs!

The morning I arrived in Hawaii, my hosts took me to a beach. I beheld majestic green mountains jutting up high above the blue Pacific, felt the soft golden sand oozing between my toes as warm waves lapped over my feet, and watched dolphins and sea turtles cavorting gracefully. The beauty, purity, lushness, and life force of the setting was nearly overwhelming. Never before had I experienced so much peace in a place and felt so enfolded in well-being. I had no idea such a haven even existed. I was home.

Two years later I moved to Hawaii—one of the best choices I have ever made. Now I am so very glad I followed my intuition and didn't blow off the conference because I didn't want to pay my expenses. I put peace before money, and that has made all the difference.

When confronted with a decision, imagine for a moment that money is not a factor, and you will see more clearly what to do. Many of us have so much negative programming and upset associated with money that the financial element of a decision clouds the decision and we become confused. If we trusted our instincts more than our fears, we would make healthier decisions in line with our true desires.

There may be times, of course, when money looms as a formidable factor in a decision and you cannot confidently move ahead with such an investment. This kind of decision is one of integrity, since you must be at peace with your choices. Simply do the best you can with what you have, and keep focusing on where your passion lives. You may be pleasantly surprised to find that at a later date your finances come up to speed with your vision, and what you once believed was but a pipe dream becomes a reality.

All successful people have had to take leaps of faith, sometimes financially. They did not wait until they had material support to follow their joy. Instead of making their choices around money, they let money revolve around their choices. When you keep joy first and money second, somehow the finances show up. Who knows, you may even have a yogi show up in your living room to remind you.

Trust thyself. Every heart vibrates to that iron string.

—Ralph Waldo Emerson

1. Name three decisions you have been thinking about or wrestling with.

   1.

   2.

   3.

2. What would you do in each situation if money were not a factor?

   1.

   2.

   3.

3. If you had an infinite supply of money, what would you be doing differently?

4. Each day spend a few minutes visualizing doing what you would do if money were not an issue. Then watch the universe support you.

AFFIRM:

The wisdom that guides me provides for me.
I make decisions from guidance, and I am well cared for.

SEVEN: DON'T BE FOOLED BY APPEARANCES

A visionary thrives

under all conditions.

FAKING FEAR OUT

To go any anywhere in the universe,
begin by knowing that you have already arrived.

—Richard Bach

During a time of lean income my money was going almost entirely to pay bills, with little left for fun. I began to feel limited, stuck in a rut, and frustrated that I did not have money for things I really enjoyed.

I began to fantasize about what I would do with money if I had it. Immediately a Mazda Miata came to mind. The Miata had just come out, and it was the rage of the auto industry. People were flocking to Mazda dealers and paying thousands of dollars over sticker price to purchase the sleek sports car. If I had the money, I thought, I would take a Miata home.

Just for fun, I decided to "act as if." I drove to the local Mazda dealer and exuberantly took a sexy convertible out for a spin on the open highway. I opened up the throttle and let the wind blow through my hair. I turned up the stereo and felt the bass beat ripple through my chest. I smelled the leather interior and rubbed it sensuously. When I returned to the showroom, I poked around under the hood and ceremoniously kicked a tire. I went through all the motions as if I was going to purchase a Miata, knowing full well that there was no way I was going to do so that day.

By the time I left the showroom, I felt exhilarated, infinitely more prosperous than when I had walked in. Playing in the realm of owning a Miata lifted my spirits and gave me a sense of possibility I had not felt for a long time. Putting myself into the experience changed my attitude; I felt that I was now on an upward tack.

Before long, my financial situation shifted and more money began to flow in. I started to find funds to do things for joy, and little by little I felt better and acted richer. But I did not end up buying a Miata. Instead, one day I drove past a Mazda dealer and spied a roaring red RX-7 convertible—the top of the Mazda sports car line, far more luxurious than the Miata. I went into the showroom and fell in love with the car. Although the RX-7 cost more than I had intended to spend, I was smitten. I snatched it up and went on to enjoy the car immensely for many years.

Looking back now, I realize that my financial turning point came the day I took the Miata for a test drive. When I had the experience of being abundant, even momentarily, the universe sent me more abundance. As my attitude changed, so did my finances.

Most people believe that if they could just become more prosperous, they would feel more prosperous. And it is so. But they do not realize that if they could just *feel* more prosperous, they would *become* more prosperous. (For a fascinating in-depth study of the Law of Reversibility, study the writings of Neville Goddard—pen name simply Neville.)

You cannot draw riches to you if you are feeling and acting poor. Likewise, you cannot be poor if you feel rich. Prime the prosperity pump by speaking and acting as if you already have what you want, or the means for it. If you can taste having what you want and slip into the experience as if it is already so, you are well on your way to having it.

Playing in your ideal realm hastens you living in that realm. Place yourself, mentally, emotionally, and/or physically, into the world you desire. Don't wait until it happens to you; you happen to it. Sign up for a photography class at the local adult school; send away for brochures about your dream vacation; volunteer as an assistant in a recording studio; ask out someone you find attractive. Suddenly a goal that once seemed outrageous now seems possible, even within your grasp.

Do not pay a lot of attention or give energy to the situation from which you are trying to remove yourself. The more you think and talk about what you don't want, the more real it seems, the more evidence you will find to keep you there, and the more public opinion you will garner to uphold that condition. Instead, talk about where you would like to be, why you want to be there, why you deserve it, and how it would feel to be there. *Your point of attention is your point of attraction.* When you invest your thoughts and feelings in an upward direction, your point of attraction becomes your dream, not your nightmare.

You are not poor unless you think you are. And if you feel poor, you can find ways to feel rich. And if you feel rich, you are rich. And if you are rich, the universe will find ways to prove you correct.

All that is necessary to break the spell of inertia and frustration is this: Act as if it were impossible to fail.

—Dorthea Brande

1. Name three things you would do if you knew you could not fail.

   1.

   2.

   3.

2. Name three things you would like to buy but do not feel you can afford at the moment.

   1.

   2.

   3.

Then call a salesperson and act as if you are shopping.

3. How much time and energy do you spend talking about how things are not working or how you are getting what you don't want?

Practice: Whenever you begin to note or complain about getting something you don't want, immediately switch to talking about what you do want instead.

AFFIRM:

I feel, think, speak, play, and live
in the world I would make my own.
Within me, I already have what I want.

THE ODDS GET EVEN

What could you not accept if you knew that all things are planned by One who has your best interests in mind?
—A Course in Miracles

After a thrilling five years with my Mazda RX-7 convertible, I decided it was time to sell the car. I put an ad in the newspaper and the next day I received a call from an interested woman. We made an appointment to meet the following afternoon in the parking lot of a local restaurant.

I had the car detailed and proudly set out for our meeting in my spotless shiny car. On my way to the restaurant, I glanced at the electric gauge and saw that the needle was dipping rapidly. This couldn't be happening! The RX-7 had been mechanically outstanding for five years, and on the very day I was to sell it, the car's electrical system was shutting down. Engine failure was imminent, and I prayed to at least make it to the restaurant.

I eked along until the restaurant was in sight, with seconds until stall. Then the unbelievable occurred: the moment I entered the parking lot, the car died and I literally rolled to a halt in a space next to the one where my potential buyer was waiting. What are the odds of this happening? If the car had died a minute earlier, I wouldn't have made it. A minute later, and the car would have failed during her test drive.

My buyer was pacing back and forth, frantic and angry. Because the car's clock had slowed down I was twenty minutes late, and she was going to be late for work. "Well, can I take the car for a test drive?" she asked, piqued.

Gulp. I wished I had something clever to say—even a decent lie. But all I could offer was the naked truth. "I hate to tell you this, but the car just died," I uttered sheepishly.

"The car *died?* But you just drove it into this spot!"

"I know I did. But the motor gave out a few seconds before I met you. I know it sounds incredible, but it's true. Something's wrong with the electrical system."

Her eyes bulged and she grunted, "Well, call me when you get it fixed!" Then she dashed into her car and peeled out in a huff.

This was too weird to be true. The universe has a strange sense of humor.

I phoned for a tow truck, and soon my beautiful detailed convertible was hanging on a hook, dragging along the highway like a side of beef. As we wended our way to the repair shop, I told myself this was just a momentary setback. The car would get fixed and somebody would buy it for a decent price. Maybe, in spite of appearances, divine order was still in force. That felt better.

Fortunately, the problem was just a broken belt, which was fixed quickly. The next day I left for a three-week trip, during which the Mazda sat in my garage. When I returned, I decided to call my potential buyer, in the remote possibility that she was still interested. She sounded calmer and more receptive. "Do you still want to look at the car?" I asked her.

"I guess so," she told me. "While you were gone I looked at two other cars, and both of them failed when I went to drive them. Isn't that weird? Maybe there's a reason."

This time, the showing went flawlessly, she loved the car, and we made a deal that netted me my desired price. She was delighted with the RX-7, and I was thrilled to sell it. The day I transferred the vehicle to her, I left a rose on the steering wheel along with a greeting card wishing her well. A month later, I received a thoughtful card from her, telling me how happy she was with her new car.

For every thing you want to sell, there is someone out there who wants to buy it. For every thing you want to buy, there is someone who needs to sell it. The universe functions in perfect balance and timing. Do not be put off by momentary setbacks. Small or large issues may come up in the course of your transaction, but if you hold the vision and remember the big picture, when all is said and done, all will be taken care of. That's divine order.

1. Can you remember a transaction that seemed to be orchestrated by a higher power operating behind the scenes? What was the lesson in the experience?

2. Is there something you want to sell, or a job or mate you seek, that is not coming as soon as you would like, or in the way you expected?

How might divine order be functioning, in spite of appearances?

3. You have probably heard the phrase "When the student is ready, the teacher appears." How might the same principle apply to business transactions and all relationships?

AFFIRM:

I place my needs in the hands of the universe,

trusting that right action is arranging everything.

Divine order is in effect, no matter the appearance.

LET THE ONE
IN LEAST FEAR LEAD

Fear knocked at the door. Faith answered. No one was there.

—Anonymous

My first excursion with my partner, Dee, was on a seminar cruise through the spectacular inside passage to Alaska. On our return voyage, our last stop in U.S. territory was the town of Ketchikan. There, I decided to mail home several boxes of books left over from our sales inventory; dispatching the books there would save us the trouble of lugging them through various ports and airports. Dee kindly offered to help me carry the few boxes off the ship.

As we approached the gangplank, a ship's officer informed us that we were not allowed to take luggage off the boat. He cited some rule about having traveled in international waters and *blah, blah, blah.* This made no sense to me, since I was a U.S. citizen mailing safe personal possessions to myself in the United States. Yet my arguments did no good, and I began to get steamed up. I demanded to see the officer's supervisor, who showed up promptly.

After hearing my case, the supervisor went to his office and returned with the news that he had phoned U.S. customs agents, who would meet us on the pier, take us to their office, and fill out necessary forms. This seemed even more ridiculous to me, and my protests grew more vehement. Just then, Dee took me aside and whispered, "Let's just listen to the fellow and go down to the pier." Although I was riled, something inside me told me to heed her suggestion. I told the supervisor I agreed, and he ordered the gate agent to let us pass.

When we arrived at the dock, I was still upset and babbling. "Just keep walking," Dee told me.

"What about the customs agents?" I asked her.

"I promise you there will be no customs agents," she answered confidently. "I worked in the hotel industry for many years, and there are ways that supervisors handle inappropriate rules that allow them, their employees, and clients to save face. You just saw a masterful example."

Scratching my head, I looked around and saw no agents. Hoping Dee was right, we walked to the post office, mailed the boxes, and returned to the ship, where no customs agents were in sight. Her assessment of the situation was correct, and our mission was accomplished.

That day I learned a crucial lesson that will make a *huge* difference in your life if you practice it: *Let the one in least fear lead.* Because Dee had a cooler head about the situation, she was in a better position to intuit our avenue to success. If it had been up to me, I might have continued to challenge the ship's staff and never gotten anywhere. But because Dee was less clouded by fear, she was more qualified to lead at that moment.

In any partnership, business, team, or relationship, the one in least fear is the most qualified to lead. If someone is angry, upset, or disconnected from their sense of well-being, that person is in the least effective position to create a positive result. The person who is the most relaxed, clear-minded, and who holds the highest vision of possibilities should lead the way and represent the partnership or company. At various times your roles may be reversed, and the other partner or another team member may embody the required strength and faith; then that person will be the most effective leader.

You can apply this principle to internal choices, as well. I met a church minister who had just assumed her post. Her first act in her new position was to sit down with several board members and review the church constitution. Their mission, as directed by her, was to remove any and all elements of the constitution that were motivated by fear and mistrust, leaving only those elements motivated by positive vision and empowerment. The committee eventually reduced the bylaws from forty pages to eighteen. The other twenty-two pages were fear-driven and unnecessary. The bylaws that remained were inspiring and matched the true teachings of her church. In this case, the ones in least fear were the eighteen healthy pages.

As long as one partner or team member remains centered at any given time, you are safe. It is only when both or all of you lose your peace that you are in danger. *A Course in Miracles* tells us that in a relationship all that is required is that one of you remains sane at any given time. The sanity or clarity of one person can lead both or all of you through and out of a storm.

When I speak at certain personal growth institutions, one person is assigned to "hold the space" for the seminar. This person sits quietly off to one side of the meeting room and meditates or prays for the success of the program. While other people are laughing, weeping, joyful, or upset, this person has one job: to be at peace. This person, though often unknown and unobserved by most participants, makes a major contribution to our event.

There is one among you or within you who is not afraid. Let that fearless one guide, and you will remain safe and be successful.

1. Consider a choice, crossroads, or response required for your relationship, business, or team.

Which persons are most fearful or upset?

Which persons are most relaxed, confident, or trusting?

How might the least fearful ones be in the best position to make a healthy choice?

2. Consider a choice, crossroads, or response required from you as an individual.

What part of you or voice within you is the most fearful or upset?

What part of you or voice within you is the most relaxed, confident, or trusting?

How might the least fearful voice or part of you be in the best position to make a healthy choice?

3. Review your past choices that were led by fear. How did they turn out?

4. Review your past choices that were led by peace. How did they turn out?

AFFIRM:

I let faith lead. Clarity is my guide.

THE WISDOM
OF WAITING

To know what you prefer instead of humbly saying "Amen"
to what the world tells you that you ought to prefer,
is to have kept your soul alive.

—Robert Louis Stevenson

During the gasoline shortage in the 1970s, I went shopping for a new car. I visited a local Honda dealer and perused the new Civic, which boasted remarkable fuel economy. After my inspection, I told the salesman that I wanted some more time to think about the car and do some comparison shopping.

"You won't have such a luxury," he warned me in an ominous voice. "Tonight, President Carter is scheduled to go on television and announce gas rationing. Tomorrow morning, there will be a long line of people vying for this car, and who knows what the price will be then."

A chill of panic rippled through me. Maybe I should snag the vehicle now, I thought, before the ravenous hordes swoop down. But something inside me said, *"Don't be intimidated by fear."* That voice felt more real and comforting than the shrill shriek of desperation. I told the salesman I would take my chances, and I calmly exited the showroom.

That night, President Carter announced gas rationing, and I continued to shop and think. A week later I decided on the Honda, and returned to the dealership. There I found the same car I had looked at, still on the showroom floor—at the same price as the previous week. The hordes had not ravaged the showroom, and sanity reigned.

As I drove my new car out of the dealership, my satisfaction was doubly sweet—once for finding the car I truly wanted, and again for acting from faith and not fear.

Never buy an item, make a business deal, or create a relationship under pressure or intimidation. Panic is the unhealthiest motivation to make a decision. You will probably regret any act you undertake under duress.

When confronted with pressure to buy or sign, take a breath and step back. Tell the salesperson you need some time to think about your decision. A salesperson with integrity will understand your reasoning and even encourage you to do so. A salesperson who relies on high-pressure tactics is waving a red flag for you *not* to make the deal.

Our media and marketing industries employ a wide repertoire of scare tactics that play on lack of consciousness in order to pressure people into buying: *Call now while supplies last; Don't be the last one on your block to . . .; Discount before midnight tonight; They're not making any more real estate; You can't afford not to do this.* Polished peddlers may further cite gloomy or sensational statistics to frighten you into forking money their way.

When you are not sure whether to purchase or act, wait until you are sure. If you see an item you may want to buy, but you have doubts, don't purchase at that moment. Walk away and see if you keep thinking about it. If so, you have a good indication to go back and get it. If you forget about it, you have your answer. *If it's not a "hell, yes!" it's a "hell, no!"*

There are times when you may encounter situations that reasonably require you to make a decision by a certain date or deadline. Or you may step into a market or situation that is moving rapidly and the item before you may not be there tomorrow. At such a moment ask your inner guide for direction, pray to act effectively, watch for signs, and then take your best shot. If your predominant energy is "yes!" and you can move ahead from a platform of joy, not fear, you are in a good position to choose well. Then step ahead confidently and expect positive results.

Consider, too, that there is often more than one right path to your goal; any one of several different approaches could work equally well. The only thing more important than the choices you make is the reason you make them. When fear is your guide, no choice is valuable. When peace and ease are at the heart of your choices, every step will bless you.

Panic is never a healthy guide for an immediate or long-term decision. In the Bible, the prophet Timothy tells us: *"God has not given us the spirit of fear; but of power, and of love, and of a sound mind."* Your sound mind is always available to you and will consistently reward you for recognizing that what truly belongs to you must come to you in the perfect way and timing.

1. Is anyone pressuring you to make a decision?

How does the pressure feel?

Do you feel obligated to act before you would choose to?

How would you be acting differently if you had less fear and more faith?

2. Are you pressuring anyone to make a decision?

Why do you want to force the issue?

How would you be acting differently if you had less fear and more faith?

3. Consider a past decision you made under duress.

What were the results?

4. Consider a past decision you made from a foundation of relaxation and clarity.

What were the results?

AFFIRM:

I choose from strength and clarity.
There is a right timing for everything,
and that which is mine shall know my face.

THE VISIONARY'S
OFFICE

Anyone can count the number of seeds in an apple,
but only God can count the number of apples in a seed.
—Source unknown

While having lunch with Dr. Frank Richelieu, minister of a large, successful church in Redondo Beach, California, I asked him how he began his career.

Dr. Richelieu smiled and told me this fascinating story: "When I first started, I had nothing—no building, no office, no congregants, no money. So I found a phone booth and wrote down the telephone number. Then I had business cards printed with that number listed as the church office. On the card I advertised our office hours as 10 a.m. to 2 p.m. daily. Every day I went to the phone booth, where I made and received calls. I even did counseling from my 'office.' Later I rented a small space for Sunday services and eventually got a real office. Over the years our congregation grew."

I gazed about the majestic sanctuary with seating for a thousand people. This highly respected ministry has enriched the lives of hundreds of thousands of people over many years. And it all began with a phone booth—and a vision.

A young fellow who wanted to make movies took a guided tour of Universal Studios. At his first opportunity, he slipped away from the tour tram and wandered around the lot until he found an empty office. He put his name on the building directory and made friends with the people in the complex. Eventually he found an editor who agreed to critique a rudimentary film he had made as a teenager. The editor liked the film and introduced the young man to studio executives, who decided to give the fellow a shot at directing. His name was Steven Spielberg.

All great achievements begin with a vision grander than the appearance at hand. Never use what has been, or what is before you, as an indication of what can be. What is within you is more real, alive, and valuable than anything the outside world shows you.

Most people accept the limits prescribed to them by their forebears or authority figures without questioning or testing them. The world seems real, solid, and formidable because many agree that it is so. Yet it is not. Great world change agents reach beyond the accepted to push the envelope of the possible. For example: the wingspan of a Boeing 747 is wider than the length of the Wright brothers' entire first flight at Kitty Hawk. If the Wright brothers believed that "if man were meant to fly, he would have wings," we might still be using only surface transportation. If Boeing believed that air flight was limited to the breadth of its inventors, we would still be flying biplanes. Neither are you bound by what anyone has done before you.

Conditions may influence consciousness, but consciousness creates conditions. Your ideas are strong electromagnets that draw equivalent circumstances. Do not wait until conditions are right for you to do what you would love. Do what you can picture in your mind, and life will imitate your inner art.

During the dramatic seventh game of the 2002 World Series between the Anaheim Angels and the New York Yankees, Angel Scott Speizio turned in a stellar performance. As he stepped up to the plate for a key at bat, the sportscaster explained that when Speizio was a child, his father used to pitch to him and told him, "Imagine that you are now batting in the seventh game of the World Series." Little did Scott or his father know at that time that one day the imaginary at-bat would become a real one—in the winning game of the Series. Keep visioning your big at-bat, and you may have your big chance to actually do it.

Artistic and scientific genius Leonardo da Vinci sketched the helicopter and submarine over four hundred years ago. Did da Vinci tap into a prophetic vision? Or was his idea simply ahead of his time? It really doesn't matter. What does matter is that he had his antenna up for greater possibilities than the known, and as such he lived on the cutting edge of human destiny and helped move it forward.

This time on the planet calls for Big Picture thinkers and individuals who can shoot arrows of focused thought into the future. That process is the most powerful when it is the most fun. Trust that your most pleasurable ideas have been seeded in you by a wisdom beyond the obvious. Then you cease to be a reactor and become a creator. And there is no greater joy than seeing what could be as if it already is.

1. What dream(s) are you waiting to act on?

What can you do today to begin to make your dream come true?

2. What creative person do you most admire?

Find any books, magazine articles, or interviews that describe that person's career, and see what you can learn from them.

3. Do you create for the pure joy of creating, or are you looking for a particular response?

How does it feel to act for sheer joy rather than seeking a response?

AFFIRM:

I think, feel, speak, and act as if
my visions and talents will change the world.
They are, and they will. I am here for a mighty purpose.

EIGHT: PIVOT ON ADVERSITY

Reframe until empowered.

SMOKE SIGNALS

Men succeed when they realize that
their failures are the preparation for their victories.

—Ralph Waldo Emerson

A lone shipwreck survivor on an uninhabited island managed to build a crude house, where he placed his meager possessions. Every day he prayed for deliverance and anxiously scanned the horizon in search of a passing ship.

One day while the fellow was cooking breakfast in his hut, he saw in the far distance the outline of an ocean liner steaming across the open sea. Immediately he ran to the beach and jumped up and down frantically, waving his arms and screaming at the top of his lungs. Alas, the ship just kept going and made no movement in his direction.

Dismayed and dejected, the man turned back to his hut and found that it had caught fire. Within the hour it burned to the ground, and all that he had was gone. The man sat on a rock and wept; surely this was the worst day of his life. That night he fell asleep depressed and dejected.

In the morning, he was awakened by a firm hand on his shoulder. He opened his eyes to see the ship's captain and a small crew. He was elated beyond words! "How did you know I was here?" he asked the captain.

"We saw your smoke signal," he answered.

There is a bigger plan for our good than meets the eye. At any given moment, we do not know how any single event fits into the big picture of our life. Sometimes what seems to be a tragedy turns out to be an integral step toward a life transformation that is far more wonderful and meaningful than what we lost. Often an obvious loss ends up being an intrinsic gain.

A Gallup survey asked people what was the worst thing that ever happened to them. Then the interviewers asked the same group what was the best thing that ever happened to them. The researchers found an 80 percent correlation between the worst things that had happened and the best. What started out to be the most terrible experience for most of these people turned out to be the most terrific. The words *terrible* and *terrific* proceed from the same root word. When strong energy moves and you resist it, the experience is terrible. If you let it lift you to greater freedom, it becomes terrific.

Very often a physical, financial, or relationship setback is the beginning of a significant course correction. The *setback* was really a *setup*. An apparent failure becomes a stepping-stone toward a new goal vastly more rewarding than the original one. Many people who lose their job, get divorced, or face a health crisis are motivated to do things they never would have done if they had simply coasted along in their old way of life. Many people settle for passionless, boring, unrewarding work or relationships, and do not realize how unhappy they are until they are jolted out of it by some unexpected event. Such jolts are the universe's way to stir you to more fulfilling living.

I met a woman who told me she had had a rude awakening. While working as a hospital technician, she injured her hand and had to leave her job. She was out of work for a long time and had to regroup to create a different livelihood.

"You've told me about the rude part," I said to her. "What about the awakening?"

She smiled and answered. "The truth is that I didn't really like my hospital job. I was always on call and often as I was driving home from work after a long day, my beeper would go off and I would have to go back. I really wanted to quit but I was afraid to. Then, when I was off work, I decided to go back to school and study psychology, which I have found much more interesting. I was also able to redevelop my relationship with my children. The injury helped me a lot more than it hurt me. I guess I didn't have the guts to ask for what I really wanted, so the universe gave me a hand."

The universe is giving you a hand, too; if you look beyond the obvious, you will find treasures invisible to the naked eye. When an apparent misfortune arises, seek the presence of the hand of love. If you have a painful pattern of finance, relationship, or health, ask what this recurring experience might be trying to get your attention to recognize. Do not be quick to interpret your position as powerless or victimized, or one of punishment. To the contrary, the experience or pattern is seeking to guide you to greater power, mastery, and self-forgiveness. Be gentle with yourself and find reasons the universe wants to love you.

The great mystical poets such as Rumi and Hafiz had ongoing ecstatic love affairs with life. Hafiz exclaimed, "It is all just a love contest and I never lose." Find love right where you stand, and you will not lose either.

1. Have you recently experienced any setback?

How could this experience be a setup for a significant awakening or life upgrade?

2. Have you had any rude awakenings?

What part was rude?

What part was the awakening?

3. How might the worst thing that ever happened to you turn out to be the best?

AFFIRM:

My good is unfolding and I open to recognize it.

I find the gift in every experience.

DO THE MATH

But in the mud and scum of things,
there always, always something sings.

—Ralph Waldo Emerson

After cashing a $500 check I drove to my favorite beach, where I left my wallet in the car's glove box, and went for a short swim. When I returned I found that someone had broken into my car and stolen my wallet and money. I had visited this beach many times and knew it to be a safe place. It was also rare that I would have so much cash with me. It seemed that all the worst possible elements had come together to work against me. Why, of all days, during that short period of time, did I get ripped off?

For several hours I churned over the loss, trying to figure out how I had attracted this experience or how I could come to peace with it. I looked at the event from many different angles, yet still I felt victimized and upset. Then I recognized I was losing my peace—a far greater loss than $500.

Finally, I found a reframe that brought me relief: I remembered that I live in an abundant universe. Through many ups and downs over my life I have always had enough money for the things I needed. The universe has consistently supported me, and would continue to do so. In the long run, I figured, this loss would not make a big difference; there would probably come a time when it would not matter at all. This line of thinking helped me to drop my upset and I felt lighter and freer.

A week later I received a phone call from a large organization planning a conference. Their featured speaker had canceled unexpectedly and they wanted me to take her place. They offered me an honorarium far greater than my usual fee, with significant benefits. I gladly accepted, and arranged another program in the vicinity. When all was said and done, my income for the weekend exceeded $15,000.

When I got home I did the math: $500 out; $15,000 in. Not a bad deal! Life was providing for me. In retrospect I believe that my willingness to let go of my immediate loss and keep an openhearted, appreciative view of the Big Picture of my life invited that huge boon to knock at my door. If I grumbled about the theft or kept repeating the story, casting myself as a victim, I would not have been an energetic match to that significant gain, and would likely not have attracted it.

When confronted with a setback, as quickly as possible find some way to look at it that helps you quit grinding about it. Do not dwell in a position of victimhood. Of course you may have feelings of loss or upset, but do your best to move to a new energetic position rapidly. Think or do something that makes you feel better, so your point of attraction is elevated to a more favorable position. Do not keep repeating your story. The story you keep repeating will keep repeating itself in your experience. Shift to your next more creative and empowering activity. Keep your head above fear, and dwell in the consciousness of the highest possibility.

Practice reframing every situation in your favor. Everything serves. Like the little cartoon figures in the Pac-Man video game, when you eat the ghosts that are trying to gobble you, you gain power to keep moving toward your goal. You are bigger than anything that haunts you. Prove this by turning every event into a stepping-stone to mastery.

Momentary losses are minuscule in comparison to the greater good that is occurring. "Evil" events represent but a minuscule, an almost imperceptible blip on the radar screen of all the things that are functioning well. Evil seems powerful only when we dwell on it. Remove your consciousness from what is not working and you will find a cornucopia of what is working. The more good you find, the more good will find you.

1. Consider a recent experience about which you feel upset. How can you reframe this experience so you feel better?

2. Is there any story of mishap you keep repeating?

Install a "victim alarm" in your subconscious mind. When something challenging occurs, give yourself no more than three times to tell about it. Each time you speak of it, move to a new level of empowerment by focusing on what you have gained through the experience. After the third time, let it go.

3. Who do you know who has a knack for turning negative experiences into blessings, or releasing them quickly?

What can you learn from this person?

AFFIRM:

I let momentary setbacks go
and I stay focused on the Big Picture of well-being.

PIVOT POWER

People are like tea bags.
They don't know their strength until they get into hot water.
— Dan McKinnon

When Southwest Airlines was the new kid on the block in 1971, the company muddled through nearly four years of legal striving to work its way into the tiny local market, bucking established carriers that resisted competition. Southwest started with four airplanes flying a small number of routes between three Texas cities. Southwest cofounder Herb Kelleher notes, "A lot of people figured us for roadkill at the time."

Before long the airline fell into financial difficulties, and the only way Southwest could survive was to sell one of its planes. If it was to stay in the black, the airline had to generate the same revenue it had created with four planes. So the company made the bold decision to fly the same number of flights with the fleet cut by 25 percent. That is how the unprecedented and now-famous twenty-minute turnaround was born.

Since that time, Southwest has become a force to be reckoned with, now the fifth largest airline in America, owning 468 airplanes flying 3,100 flights a day to fifty-eight cities. Southwest has often registered the best on-time record, best baggage handling, and fewest customer complaints. During the post–September 11 recession, Southwest was the only airline in America to turn a profit. Annually the airline receives ten times the number of applicants for its available positions.

Ultimately, adversity did not knock Southwest out of the market—it made it fly.

Rather than fighting what seems to be blocking your path, pivot on it and make it your ally. As in the martial art of aikido, you can take the energy directed against you and rechannel it to help you. Everything is energy; what you do with it is up to you.

Difficulties keep us on the cutting edge of growth and move us to levels of authority far more rewarding than if the challenge had not occurred. All evolutionary advances have resulted from novel adaptations to changes in environmental conditions. Life is not trying to hurt you; it is trying to get you to grow. As Friedrich Nietzsche wrote, "That which does not kill me makes me stronger."

Cease to view difficult situations as trouble; trouble is an interpretation, not a fact. In Arabic, the word for *problem* is translated as "another view," implying that every difficulty invites us to see from a higher perspective. Albert Einstein explained that you can never solve a problem at the same level of consciousness that created it. You must stand on higher ground. Because we are spiritual beings, the answer is always spiritual. Dr. Wayne Dyer titled a book *There's a Spiritual Solution to Every Problem*.

Practice eliminating self-defeating language from your vocabulary by replacing words of victimization with those of empowerment. *Trouble* becomes *challenge; problem* becomes *project; crisis* becomes *opportunity; failure* becomes *experience; setback* becomes *setup;* and *hit a wall* becomes *course correction*.

Thank and bless the people and situations that challenge you, for they are nudging you to greater good. At our first Mastery Training in Fiji, our group was assigned by our hotel to a meeting room on top of a hill that required transporting the entire group up and down for each gathering—quite a task. To make matters worse, we found during our first session that the room was small and hot and had poor acoustics. We were not looking forward to a week of bucking distance, elevation, size, temperature, and sound.

The next morning, as our group was gathering to ascend the hill, the hotel manager apologetically informed us that a bus had broken down on the one-lane road, and we would not be able to pass it. As an alternative he had erected an open-walled tent right on the beach, mere steps from our quarters. This meeting site turned out to be far superior to the room on the hill, with fabulous ocean views and soft breezes. The group loved our new locale, which contributed immensely to the quality of our program for the entire week. We all agreed that the broken bus was a major blessing in disguise, and we marveled at the synchronicity of its timing at the beginning of our program.

Albert Camus declared: "In the midst of winter I discovered within me an invincible summer." Your spirit is greater than any problem you encounter, and your mind can conjure creative synchronicities and solutions. In his book *Illusions,* Richard Bach notes: "Every problem comes to you with a gift in its hands." When you discover the gift—like Southwest—you are free to fly.

1. Have you ever had an enemy who turned out to be a friend?

   How did the transformation occur?

   What was your role in the shift?

2. Is there any person or situation that you now consider an enemy?

   How might you transform the situation by thinking about it in a different way?

3. Consider a challenge you might be having. How might the answer be a spiritual one?

4. Practice: Be keenly aware of the words you use to describe your experiences. Stay alert to your tendency to use words couched in victimization or disempowerment. The moment you begin to speak such language, stop and substitute another word with a neutral or positive connotation.

AFFIRM:

I embrace challenge as an invitation to greater success.
Difficulties empower me toward superior strength.

SOMEONE WILL
SAY YES

Be like a postage stamp. Stick to it until you get there.

—Harvey Mackay

At the end of a business trip, I had to change the date of my flight back to Hawaii. Since my original ticket was nonchangeable, I decided I would redeem frequent flyer miles for the new flight. I called the airline to check if seats were available on my desired flight, and I was told I should have no problem.

I arrived at the airport at 8 a.m. to make the 9 a.m. flight. When I reached the check-in desk, however, the agent told me, "I'm sorry, sir, you can't use your mileage today. This is a blackout day for frequent flyer miles redemption." I asked the agent how much it would cost to pay for the flight, and the price was, well, humorous.

Hmmm. There must be a way, I thought. I walked twenty feet across the lobby to the pay phone and called the airline. I told the reservations agent I wanted to redeem miles for the 9 a.m. flight, and she gave me the same response as the counter agent. I thanked her, hung up, dialed again, and told the next agent my request. She also told me that I would not be able to fly today on miles. I hung up, dialed again, and told the next agent my request. Her response was different: "Sure, I'd be happy to get you onto that flight, sir." Bingo. An hour later I was in the air, jetting my way home. With a smile.

If you ask enough people, eventually someone will say yes. If something is really important to you, don't stop at the first no. Or the second. Or the third. You may hear no three, ten, or thirty times before you get your yes, but you will get your yes. Someone out there will resonate with your intention and help you create it.

Rejections, even multiple rejections, are not necessarily an indication of the lack of worth of your project. They may simply be indications of a mismatch of the applicant and rejecter. Or lack of good taste on the part of the person denying your request. Some of the greatest works of art and literature were overlooked by many people. In his lifetime, Vincent van Gogh sold but one painting, for a pittance. In recent years, one of his paintings sold for $135 million—the highest price ever paid for an oil painting. The film *Dead Poets Society* was turned down by eleven studios, *twice* each; the movie went on to receive seven Academy Award nominations, including Best Picture and Best Actor. The blockbuster parable *Jonathan Livingston Seagull* was rejected by seventeen publishers before Macmillan acquired it, and went on to sell many millions of copies. And on and on and on.

My friend Gudrun Cable had a dream to create a theme hotel based on great writers and their books. She found an old hotel for sale on the magnificent windswept shore of Newport, Oregon, and applied for a loan to buy it. Her request was rejected. She went to another bank and was turned down by them as well. But she did not stop there. Gudrun went to thirty banks before one said yes. But one did say yes. Then she enrolled her friends with a deal: if they would each decorate a room according to the life and times of their favorite author, she would trade them for a two-week vacation at the hotel for five years. A number of Gudrun's friends agreed, and she went on to create one of the most unique hotels in the world. On the opening day of the Sylvia Beach Hotel, over two thousand people came to visit. Now the hotel is thriving and creating a memorable experience for all of its guests. Thank goodness, Gudrun did not stop after a few noes!

The responses you receive from the outer world reflect your internal beliefs. If you have doubts about yourself, others will have doubts about you. If you believe in yourself and your project, so will someone out there. Your process of bringing your vision to life is an exercise in self-belief. If you have strong internal (yet subconscious) self-rejections, you will receive strong external rejections. If you have mixed feelings, you will get mixed results. When you know for sure that you deserve yes, some-one will say yes. When you have faith in yourself and recognize you de-serve it all, the universe has no choice but to match your knowing.

The universe is a big "Yes!" machine. All of life is an affirmation of what can be. Your role is not to try to fight to make things happen, but to line up with where the "Yes!" lives. The moment you do, doors will open and arms will receive you. You have a seat on your flight home if you are willing to claim it.

1. Describe a project you had to persevere to achieve.

   How did the process reflect your inner beliefs and their evolution from doubt to confidence?

2. Is there a project, dream, or goal that you are now being called to persevere to accomplish?

   How might your obstacles be reflecting any inner doubts or mixed intentions you have about this project?

   Why do you want this goal to come to pass?

   Why do you deserve it?

AFFIRM:

My talents and visions are worth resounding approval.
I say yes to myself, and life says yes to me.

HOW LONG
IT TOOK

Great things are not done by impulse,
but by a series of small things brought together.

—Vincent van Gogh

In the charming French resort town of Nice, an American woman named Joan was shopping in the outdoor market one morning when she saw an energetic elderly man who resembled the renowned artist Pablo Picasso, carrying a sketch pad under his arm. With trepidation, Joan approached the man and asked him, "Excuse me, sir, but are you Pablo Picasso?"

"That's right," he answered softly.

Excitement exuded through every pore of Joan's being. "I don't mean to disturb you," she told him, bubbling, "but I am one of your biggest fans. Is there any way you would be willing to take a few minutes and do a simple sketch of me? I'd be happy to pay you."

Picasso stepped back a foot or two, studied the woman's features, and then answered with a smile, "Yes, I will."

Joan swooned. The two walked to a nearby sidewalk café, where they claimed a quiet table. Picasso opened his pad, reached into his jacket pocket for a small piece of charcoal, and went to work. Fifteen minutes later he turned the pad around and showed Joan his finished work. It was spectacular—an authentic Picasso, of her!

Joan took the portrait, embraced it, and thanked the master profusely. She opened her purse, took out her checkbook, and asked, "How much will that be?"

"Five thousand dollars," Picasso answered in a matter-of-fact manner.

Joan's jaw dropped. "Five thousand dollars? But, sir, with all due respect, the picture took you only fifteen minutes to draw!"

"No, madam," he answered calmly. "You don't understand. The picture took me *eighty years* and fifteen minutes to draw."

Everything you know and do represents the sum of everything you have done and learned. Every triumph and failure you have undergone, or have observed in the lives of others, has contributed to your wisdom and skill. You stand on the shoulders of all the lessons that have brought you to this point.

When offering your services or negotiating your fee or contract, attribute proper value to the experience that has seasoned you. Even if you are inexperienced in a certain field, you can likely transfer the expertise you have gained in another arena. A good salesperson can sell anything. If you know how to sell cars, selling computers is just a matter of learning the details of the industry. Data is easier to learn than skill. Once you have the skill, you own it for a lifetime.

A famous story tells of a company that needed a boiler repaired. The manager called in a repairman and explained the problem to him. The fellow surveyed the situation, went to his toolbox, and took out a screwdriver and a screw. He walked to the boiler, opened a small door, replaced the screw, and adjusted it. Immediately the boiler began to work.

On his way out, the repairman presented the manager with a bill for $100. "One hundred dollars?" exclaimed the manager. "All you did was turn a screw."

"Yes," answered the repairman. "One dollar for the screw and ninety-nine dollars for knowing which screw to turn."

Employers or clients pay you something for your actions, but they pay you more for your consciousness. People who get paid the most are those whose decisions affect the largest number of people. Anyone can dish out popcorn at a movie theater concession, but fewer people can design a popcorn display that will attract lots of people. Your ideas are worth more than your deeds. So rather than doing more, think more. Feel more. Be more. As you fine-tune your connection to your creative source, you will further your career far more rapidly than by working longer hours or sweating harder at a job you don't love. Knowledge is power, and experience builds knowledge.

Even if you are inexperienced in a field, if you know how to tap into the bank account of wisdom you have built over your life (some would say many lives), you have access to phenomenal resources. How long does success take? As long as it takes for you to reach into yourself. Respect yourself and charge in proportion to the wealth of your wisdom, and you will honor yourself, your work, and your clients.

1. What have been your most significant jobs, and what skills did you learn from them?

2. What have been your most significant relationships, and what skills did you learn from them?

3. What have been your most significant life experiences, and what skills did you learn from them?

4. Do you believe you are being paid well for the wisdom and skills you have developed through your life and career experiences?

   If not, what fee or salary do you believe would be commensurate with your level of skill and experience?

5. If you are changing or considering a change in your career or your world of relationships, describe how all of your experiences qualify you to succeed in your next step and be rewarded well for it.

AFFIRM:

I am the best I have ever been. I deserve to be paid and given rewards commensurate with my abilities and experience. I live on the cutting edge of my skill, success, and destiny.

NINE: BE EXCELLENT TO EACH OTHER

Make people your business and

people will make your business.

ISNESS IS
YOUR BUSINESS

Success usually comes to those
who are too busy to be looking for it.

—Henry David Thoreau

Not long after my mother passed away, a woman named Carol invited me to present a seminar for her personal development organization. "What is your fee?" Carol asked me. At that time I was charging $500 or 50 percent of the net income, whichever was greater. As I considered that Carol's group would not be large enough for the percentage deal to be significant, I quoted her a flat fee of $500.

A week later I received a sample flyer advertising the event. To my surprise, Carol had listed a ticket price of $25 in advance and $30 at the door—nearly twice the going rate for seminars at that time. I felt my gut contract as I considered the program overpriced and I expected few people would show up. I picked up the telephone to advise Carol to lower the ticket fee, but a strong inner voice stopped me. The voice stated: "The price she is charging is not your business. Your job is to show up and offer insight and inspiration. Don't try to boss the money. Just let her do as she has chosen." My guidance was so compelling that I surrendered to it and I let the issue go.

Several weeks before the program, I phoned Carol to find out how registration was going. "Great!" she informed me excitedly. "We have fifty tickets sold." After we hung up, I went to my calculator. *Hmmm.*

If I had quoted her my regular contract based on the percentage split, I would be making more than $500. I wondered if I should call her back and renegotiate. Then that annoying yet authoritative voice spoke again: "A deal is a deal. The ticket price is not your business. Your job is to show up and shine. Just let it go and quit complaining."

Okay, okay, I can let go.

A week before the event, I received a call from Carol. "Ticket sales are doing very well!" she reported gleefully. "We have one hundred tickets sold!" Great, I thought, as I got out my calculator. If I had quoted my regular deal, I would be making *a lot* more than $500. Maybe I should give her a call and ask to up my percentage. Again spoke the voice: "Just let this be. You are a healer, not a dealer. Fulfill your function, and everything else will be taken care of."

Okay, okay. I will go along with the game.

When I showed up at the program, I found 137 people in the audience. Immediately my mental calculator swung into action and again I started to kick myself for not negotiating a better deal. How unfair, I thought, that Carol should make the lion's share of the income, and I receive a small percentage. One final time the voice told me: "All is well. Be grateful you have a good crowd. Stand and deliver."

I put aside my concerns and presented the program to the best of my ability. Many people were uplifted and inspired, and a woman with cancer experienced a significant shift. By the end of the evening, I felt utter peace and was very satisfied with the event.

After the crowd departed, Carol sat down with me to settle the finances. She took out her checkbook and told me, "We did really well tonight. I think it's only fair that we go 50/50 on the net." Then Carol handed me a check for $1,100—the largest fee I had earned for a lecture until that time! I was thrilled.

The next day I received a final bill in the mail from my mother's doctor. You can imagine my surprise when I opened the envelope to find the outstanding balance was $1,100—exactly the amount of my income from the previous evening's program. Grateful for the bounty, I penned him a check and realized that a hand greater than my own had orchestrated the entire experience.

Isness is your business. Simply be who you are, do what you do best, be where you are called by joy, and let life work its magic on your behalf.

1. Is there any situation in which you are letting money distract you from your higher purpose?

How would you be feeling or acting differently if you kept your purpose before dollars?

2. Is there any situation in which you are trying to boss all the details, and feeling worse for it?

How would you be acting and feeling differently if you left the details to a Higher Power?

3. What is your "main thing," the attribute of life you value most and want to keep first?

4. Who are you and how do you feel and act when you stay true to your personal mission?

Note a situation in which you kept the main thing first, and how it turned out.

AFFIRM:

Isness is my business.
The more I keep the main thing the main thing,
the better everything works out.

A PROPER
CUP OF TEA

Not in time, place, or circumstances, but in the man lies success.
—Charles B. Rouss

In a little town near my home, a fellow named Jacques opened a restaurant at a seemingly jinxed location with a long history of failed eateries. Within a few months Jacques' Bistro was booming. It was easy to see why. Jacques took pride in his menu, priced his meals attractively, created a cozy ambiance, hired classy waitresses, and schmoozed amiably with customers. Before long, Jacques' Bistro developed a glowing, far-reaching reputation and became the hot spot in town for dining and social gatherings.

After several years of increasing success, Jacques' landlord raised his rent sky high. Jacques was unwilling to pay the inflated price, so he sold the business to another entrepreneur. For a while Jacques' customers kept coming, hoping the dining experience Jacques had instituted would be carried on in high style. But soon they discovered the new owner did not have the pizzazz of his predecessor. Although the new management tried to capitalize on Jacques' reputation, the atmosphere, food, and service were a far cry from the legendary Jacques'. The café plummeted quickly and, in the bistro that once bulged at the seams every night, but a few hapless diners could be found. After a few months, the new restaurant closed its doors.

Then a stroke of good luck befell the town: Jacques opened another restaurant across the street from his former location. Word spread, and within a few weeks the place was burgeoning with happy customers. Now, years later, Jacques' reputation attracts customers from all over the world. And so the legend of Jacques' continues, to the delight of his loyal audience.

A Chinese maxim declares: "If you can serve a cup of tea properly, you can do anything." Once you know how to succeed in a chosen field (or any field), you take your ability with you wherever you go. Conditions mean little to one who is the master of his or her craft. Masters are not thwarted by conditions—they create them.

When I was a teenager, I took up playing the saxophone and joined a rock band. After tooting my new instrument for a while, I still could not get a good tone out of it. I complained to my parents, who spoke to my saxophone teacher about getting me a better horn.

Then one night while our band was playing for a dance, a fellow emerged from the audience and asked if he could sit in with the band and play a song on my sax. Sure, I told him, and handed him the horn. The moment he began to play I could hardly believe my ears—this fellow extracted an *incredibly beautiful* tone from the sax. I sat listening, rapt, with my jaw open. Humbled, I realized there was nothing wrong with the sax—I just didn't know how to play it. The limit was not in the horn; it was in the mind.

If you can learn to do one thing well, you can learn to do all things well. That is why it is so important to give 100 percent of your presence and attention to whatever you do. Nothing is too menial to practice excellence. If you learn to do seemingly unimportant daily tasks with love and quality, when it comes time to achieve big things, you will have all the skill and experience you need.

My friend Millie operated a successful motivational school. Once, after I met with Millie, she told me she was off to teach the first class in a new semester.

"Good luck!" I told her.

"Thanks," she replied, "but I don't need luck. I am programmed to succeed."

Like Millie, Jacques, and my guest sax player, you and I can program ourselves to succeed. Ingenious people take what they have and make what they want. Whatever they touch turns to success because they apply inner skills to outer circumstances. Great thinkers often demonstrate genius in a variety of disciplines. Leonardo da Vinci was an exemplar artist, scientist, and mathematician. Benjamin Franklin excelled at writing, printing, science, and politics. Our present day Steve Jobs developed the Macintosh computer, established Pixar Animation Studios, and created the iPod. When you know how to do one thing well, you enhance your ability to do all things well.

The task before you now is your opportunity to practice excellence. No role is too obscure or too overwhelming to apply your innate genius. You cannot be limited or stopped by your landlord, the economy, your history, astrology, or any other circumstance. If need be, like Jacques, you will just pick yourself up and start over on the other side of the street, where all who understand and appreciate you will find and support you.

1. What activities do you regularly succeed at?

   What is it that you do or bring to these activities that makes them successful?

2. Name someone who succeeds at whatever they touch, or has a particular skill that succeeds wherever they apply it.

   What can you learn from them?

3. How can you take the task before you, even if it is not your ultimate goal, and maximize your presence with it and the results you create?

AFFIRM:

I have the power to succeed under all circumstances.

My goals come to life because I bring my full presence to them.

GOOD LEMONADE

Try not to become a man of success.
Rather become a man of value.

—Albert Einstein

While I was teaching a few yoga classes a week in an evening school, I decided to branch out and make yoga my full-time profession. So I set out on a massive publicity campaign. I opened the phone book and scoured the Yellow Pages for every health club, community center, and adult school in my area. I made lots of cold calls, had flyers printed, and sent out query letters.

After a great deal of hustling I landed two new classes: one in a community center and the other in a small hotel health spa. The number of responses to my blitz seemed small relative to the energy I had put out, but I figured it was a start. Eagerly I anticipated my new venues.

A few days before the community center class was to begin, I received a call from their administrator informing me they had to cancel due to low enrollment. I was disappointed. I took a breath and consoled myself that at least I was set for the health spa class.

When that class began, I realized that the manager had no concept of what yoga was about and little respect for it. He assigned us to a tiny space in the midst of the area where bodybuilders were working out on the Nautilus equipment. My students had to position themselves on the floor around the machines and dodge people walking over them on their way to exercise. During our final relaxation period, a time devoted to quiet serenity, the weight lifters would make snide comments. The class was far from what I had envisioned. I finished the course and had no desire to return. I wondered where I had gone wrong.

Around that time, my friend Frank Asch gave me a copy of his children's book *Good Lemonade*. The story is about a boy named Hank who sets up a lemonade stand in front of his house. During his first few days on the job, Hank attracts only a handful of customers, and no one returns. So he tries all kinds of gimmicks and come-ons to attract customers: he offers discounts, paints the cups, and hires two go-go girls to dress up as lemons. After a week of finagling, Hank still makes only a few sales.

Then Hank discovers that another kid has set up a lemonade stand down the block, and he has a long line of customers every day. Hank decides to stand in the long line to find out why the other kid is selling so much lemonade. When he finally tastes the lemonade, his eyes light up. It is really *good lemonade*! Hank dashes home and mixes his own lemonade with fresher lemons and a little more sugar. The next day he finds a long line of kids at his own stand, waiting for their cup of good lemonade.

There was my lesson: *Success is less about manipulating and more about excellence.* I decided that instead of spending a lot of time, energy, and money trying to market myself, I would take the few classes I was already teaching and make them the best classes I could offer. That felt a lot better, and my joy returned.

The results were miraculous. Within a few months the classes were overflowing thanks to word of mouth. Soon I began to receive invitations to teach classes in other school districts. One district asked me to fill in for a yoga teacher who had unexpectedly canceled for an in-service training day. Subsequently the district hired me for ongoing classes for their teachers, which continued for many years. My self-marketing gyrations did not pay off, but my good lemonade did.

I heard about a small-town, family-owned furniture store that was successful over several generations. One day the owner's son observed a customer come to his father and demand that he repair a chair she had bought at the store a while ago. As the son watched his father examine the chair, he noticed an emblem indicating that the chair had been bought at another store. Yet the father said nothing and accepted the chair for repair. When the son asked his father why he had agreed to fix the chair, his father answered, "She will buy her next piece of furniture here."

Success is built not on come-ons but on quality, attention to detail, and integrity. It is about customer care, follow-up, and joy in the process. While promotion is important, your satisfied customers do your best advertising.

When you make excellence and service your highest priorities, your clients will recognize the depth of your investment. Integrity is the magnet that attracts success beyond volumes of flashy promotion. While it is important to let people know about what you do, it is more important to let people know how much you can give them once they show up.

1. Are you putting more energy into promotion of your business than maintaining or improving the quality of your product or service?

How could you shift more of your energy from selling to serving?

2. Name three businesses you keep returning to patronize.

1.

2.

3.

What is there about these businesses that keeps you coming back?

3. How do high-end businesses such as Porsche, Gucci, and Rolex charge so much for their products and still have customers flocking to purchase them?

AFFIRM:

I imbue my work with my heart, soul, energy, and essence.

I keep excellence and service first,

and my integrity attracts success.

THE CLEANING LADY

*To awaken each morning with a smile brightening my face; to
greet the day with reverence for the opportunities it contains; to
hold ever before me, even in the doing of little things, the
Ultimate Purpose toward which I am working; to meet men and
women with laughter on my lips and love in my heart; to be gentle, kind, and courteous through all the hours; to approach the
night with weariness that ever woos sleep and the joy that comes
from work well done—this is how I desire to waste wisely my days.*

—Thomas D. Carlyle

While you may be investing diligent effort to do your job well,
there is another aspect of your work that is equally (and perhaps more) important. This poignant anecdote (from an unknown
source) captures the essence of right livelihood:

> During my second month of nursing school, our professor gave
> us a pop quiz. I was a conscientious student and had breezed
> through the questions, until I read the last one:
> "What is the first name of the woman who cleans the school?"
> Surely, this was some kind of joke. I had seen the cleaning
> woman several times. She was tall, dark-haired, and in her fifties.
> But how would I know her name?
> I handed in my paper, leaving the last question blank. Before
> class ended, one student asked if the last question would count
> toward our quiz grade. "Absolutely," answered the professor. "In

your careers you will meet many people. All are significant. They deserve your attention and care, even if all you do is smile and say hello."

I've never forgotten that lesson. I also learned her name was Dorothy.

The secret of building your business it to build your relationships. You may be able to generate some immediate gains by manipulation, but unless you build healthy, respectful relationships with your clients and associates, your gains will be short-lived. The most successful people do not set out to simply make money. They seek more deeply to make friends.

When you build your success on relationships, it filters through everyone in your organization. Once when I returned a rental car I was in a hurry to get to the airport. The attendant who checked the car in, however, captured my attention. A Hispanic fellow with a wide smile, Manuel asked me, "So, did you like the car, sir?" "Yes," I told him, "It was fine." "That's good," Manuel answered, "You come back again and we will give you a nice car again." I was stunned. Here was a fellow who was seemingly on the lowest rung of the company's totem pole, yet he took responsibility for customer satisfaction as if he were the CEO. I have rented from that company ever since that day.

I heard about a hotel CEO who took one day a month to do the job of a different employee. One day he registered guests at the front desk; another day he served food in the restaurant; another day he changed linens with the chambermaids. He wanted to know firsthand the world he was administering through the eyes of those who were living in that domain many hours a day. In the process, he made friends and developed compassion that made him a successful and effective leader.

I received a glowing letter from a woman who had benefited from one of my books. I appreciated her taking the time and caring to write, and sent her an acknowledgment. Several years later she attended my Mastery Training and reported that she came because she was impressed by the fact that I answered her personally. The tuition for that program was approximately $1,000. From a business standpoint, one might say that my personal response to the woman resulted in a thousand-dollar income. Certainly I did not respond to her for that reason; yet when I kept caring at the top of my priority list, the universe cared for my material needs.

We live in a time when many people, businesses, and corporations have been so distracted by material success that the human element is sadly placed on a back burner. At the extreme, some businesses are quite devoid of heart and consumed by the bottom line. Yet what line is more bottom than giving and receiving kindness? Voltaire asked: "What are we here for if not to make life easier for each other?" The miracle is that when we make life easier for each other, we make it easier for ourselves.

Make people your business, and people will make your business.

1. Can you think of one worker low on the chain of power in a company who has made a difference in your workday or life?

How does that person represent the attitude and energy that filters down from the higher echelons of the corporation?

2. Which group of people do you think is closer to peace: CEOs of corporations, or shuttle bus drivers?

3. Do you take the time to connect with your doorman, postal clerk, toll booth operator, or highway construction crew?

Who in your arena of work or daily activities could you acknowledge more or get to know better?

How might you thank or honor them?

AFFIRM:

I honor the spirit of those I work with.
I build my business by building relationships.

HOW TO BLESS
THE IRS

If you're not praisin', you're crazin'.

—Jorge Tortuga

Whenever Alice wrote a check, she penned a note of good wishes on the memo line. One April, as she was paying her bills, Alice came to the check due to the Internal Revenue Service for her tax payment. She stopped for a moment and wondered: "Do I really want to bless the IRS? Would anyone there appreciate the gift?"

After some reflection, Alice decided that there are no exceptions to the law of circulating well-being. "Perhaps," she reasoned, "the IRS can use blessing as much as the other people and companies I am paying—maybe more. So Alice took her pen and inscribed on the memo line of her check: *Peace and joy be with you.*

The following month when Alice was reconciling her checking account, she found the canceled check she had sent to the IRS. On the back of the check, below the institutional stamp, she was amazed to read these words, written by hand: *And with you, too.*

Somehow Alice's blessing found its way to a real person who appreciated it. Consider what a gift this was to the person who received it. The IRS is probably not the most delightful place to work. Hardly anyone enjoys paying taxes, and I suspect that IRS employees are not the recipients of many blessings from their constituents. Can you imagine the pleasant surprise of the person who processed the check?

Perhaps it changed their entire day. Perhaps that person went on to offer some extra kindness, caring, or forgiveness to the next person they dealt with. I am certain that Alice's blessing went a long way.

The situations we encounter are templates upon which we craft our intentions. Any activity in life can be lifted to the level of blessing. Every moment, we make the choice between love and fear. Acting from fear turns the world into hell. When you choose love, you bring the world closer to heaven. The choice is yours.

Paying taxes or making any other obligatory payment is a good opportunity to practice keeping your energy high and not giving your power away. When you get upset about money, you cut off its flow to you and through you. Relaxing and staying light opens the door for more to come. Offering blessing is a powerful way to prove this principle. It is said, "You cannot outgive God." The more you give, the more God gives to you to give.

Money takes on whatever purpose you ascribe to it. If someone wants to fight with you over money, you have a choice as to whether or not you will go there with them. People who want to fight can always find a reason, and money is something lots of people agree is worth fighting over. At the same time, people who want to create harmony can always find a way to do so, and money transactions are wonderful opportunities to celebrate abundance.

I know a woman who had this sentiment printed on her checks:

> *Every dollar I spend enriches the economy,*
> *blesses everyone it touches,*
> *and returns to me multiplied.*

Behold a powerful affirmation! What a sharp contrast to fear and resistance.

I used to bristle when I received a credit card bill. I would go over each item and either wish I hadn't bought that article or begrudge the vendor the high price. Then one day I decided I would use my credit card bill as an exercise in appreciation. As I looked at each entry, I mentally thanked the vendor for providing me with an article or service that I wanted or needed. Very quickly I realized that all of these people and companies had helped me immensely. Then I wrote a check with joy and appreciation. Quickly, more money began to flow to me. When I primed the pump with gratitude, the universe sent more my way.

These principles really work. A sage once advised: "Be gentle with everyone, for everyone is fighting an inner battle." No act of kindness is too small or goes unnoticed. Practice using money as a vehicle of blessing, and you will be the recipient of every blessing you give.

1. Do you make payments easily and joyfully, or do you feel a sense of loss, fear, or resentment?

2. Is there anyone whom you begrudge paying money to?

How does your resentment affect your relationship with that person?

How does your resentment affect your sense of abundance and your ability to receive the good you desire?

3. How might you reframe such payment(s) to leave you feeling better?

How do you think an attitudinal shift toward blessing might affect your prosperity?

3. Practice writing a short note of thanks or blessing on the checks you write. What phrase would it most empower you to inscribe?

AFFIRM:

I use every situation to practice blessing.
There are no exceptions to the power and presence of love.

THE ATTITUDE
OF GRATITUDE

Almost the whole world is asleep. Everybody you know, everyone you see, everyone you talk to. Only a few people are awake, and they live in constant total amazement.

—from the film *Joe Versus the Volcano*

The secret of the greatest wealth is no secret—but since so few people know and practice it, true riches remain beyond the reach of the masses. The easiest, most direct, and most rewarding way to increase your wealth is to be thankful.

In *The Gospel According to Jesus,* Stephen Mitchell adapts a marvelous Zen parable from Zenkei Shibayama's *A Flower Does Not Talk:*

There lived a woman named Sono, whose devotion and purity of heart were respected far and wide. One day a fellow Buddhist, having made a long trip to see her, asked, "What can I do to put my heart at rest?"

Sono said, "Every morning and every evening, and whenever anything happens to you, keep on saying, 'Thank you for everything. I have no complaint whatsoever.' "

The man did as he was instructed for a whole year, but his heart was still not at peace. He returned to Sono crestfallen. "I've said your prayer over and over, and yet nothing in my life has changed; I'm still the same selfish person as before. What should I do now?"

Sono immediately said, "Thank you for everything. I have no complaint whatsoever."

On hearing these words, the man was able to open his spiritual eye, and returned home with a great joy.

Gratitude, like the heart, is a muscle; the more you use it, the more powerful it becomes. The more you find to appreciate, the more you will find to appreciate.

I learned about the power of gratitude from my ten-year-old goddaughter, Shanera. One afternoon as I drove Shanera to her family's new residence, we turned off the highway onto a dirt road that led to her house. My heart sank to see that she and her parents were living in an old school bus in a field.

As Shanera showed me around her family's quarters, I felt sad that this little girl whom I loved so much was growing up in such a shoddy environment. When my eyes fell upon rusted seams on the metal walls, cracked windows, and a leaking roof, I realized that her family had fallen into bare subsistence living. I wanted to rescue her from such a barren plight.

Looking up at me with her big brown eyes, Shanera took me by the hand and led me up a makeshift staircase to a small wooden addition that had been superimposed over the roof of the bus. This was her room. It was in the same condition as the rest of the place, just barely livable. The only attractive piece of decor I noticed was a colorful tapestry hanging over one wall.

"How do you feel about living here?" I asked Shanera, waiting for a glum response.

Instead, to my surprise, her face lit up. "I love my wall!" she giggled.

I was stunned. The child was not kidding. She enjoyed the place because of this colorful wall. Shanera found a touch of heaven in the midst of hell, and this is what she chose to focus on. She was happy.

I drove home in a state of awe. This ten-year-old saw her life through the eyes of appreciation, and that made all the difference. I began to consider all the things in my life that I had complained about. In my preoccupation with what wasn't there, I was missing what *was* there.

Appreciate what you have before asking for more. If you are not happy with what you have, you will not be happy with what you get. This is not to say that you must make believe you are happy when you are not; or put up with abuse; or trudge through life with a martyrlike attitude of self-sacrifice. It is to say that those who find good where they stand are the most likely to find greater good where they next stand. When you focus on what makes your heart soar, your heart will soar even farther.

Gratitude is a prayer that goes far beyond asking, for in giving thanks you affirm your riches. It is the most powerful meditation of a lifetime. Those who practice thankfulness are the happiest people in the world, and, by their own discovery, the richest.

You are not a beggar at the table of life.
You are the honored guest.

—Emmanuel

1. Make a list of all the reasons *Why I am the luckiest person in the world.*

2. Write the names of the seven people in your life whom you most appreciate, and what about them you appreciate. Then telephone, e-mail, or write them and tell them.

3. Write down a few situations in your life that you find challenging, and then find something to appreciate about each one.

AFFIRM:

Thank you for everything. I have no complaint whatsoever.

WEALTH WISDOM KEYS

WEALTH WISDOM KEY	MEMORY HOOK
1. Abundance is natural.	*Always enough.*
2. Life will give you as much as you are open to receive.	*You get what you let.*
3. Do what brings you life.	*Passion pays.*
4. Let it be easy. Struggle is not required.	*Don't sweat the petty stuff and don't pet the sweaty stuff.*
5. Generate, replicate, circulate.	*Your economy depends on you.*
6. Moving wealth out moves wealth in.	*Circulate, circulate, circulate.*
7. A visionary thrives under all conditions.	*Don't be fooled by appearances.*
8. Reframe until empowered.	*Pivot on adversity.*
9. Make people your business and people will make your business.	*Be excellent to each other.*

ACKNOWLEDGMENTS

A brilliant teacher once told me, "Gratitude is as close to heaven as you get on earth." Expressing it invites others to join you there.

In my own journey to understand *Relax into Wealth* principles, some wonderful and astute friends and colleagues have supported me immensely. Their powerful consciousness is woven into the fabric of this book. Their energy and caring have contributed to enhancing the lives of our readers, and I want to appreciate and acknowledge them here.

My deepest thanks to:

My amazing beloved partner, Dee Winn, who has journeyed with me through many life lessons in recognizing prosperity, obvious and hidden, and supported me to remember how good it can get. Dee's wise and radiant spirit helps me remember daily how blessed I am to walk side by side with one so gifted in so many ways.

Kathy McDuff and Rich Lucas, for their unswerving friendship and kind and efficient care for those who find their way to our books and seminars. I am ever more inspired by Kathy's and Rich's heartfelt dedication to our natural legacy and the native people who embody it.

Michael Ebeling and Kristina Holmes, of Ebeling and Associates, who believe in me and this work and whose efforts to bring this book to you via the perfect publisher have been stellar and noble.

Joel Fotinos, Mitch Horowitz, and all the good people at Tarcher/Penguin, who are a match to the principles and energy of *Relax into*

Wealth and recognize the potential gift to our readers. What a blessing to work with a publisher and editors who get it and live it!

You, the reader, whose openness and eagerness to live the good life draw forth this material into expression and application.

All the dear people whose paths have been woven with mine, and who, with a word, glance, or courageous deed, have inspired me to recognize and remember that life is a gift and we can have it all if we choose it.

ABOUT THE AUTHOR

Alan Cohen is the author of twenty popular inspirational books, including the best-selling *The Dragon Doesn't Live Here Anymore,* the award-winning *A Deep Breath of Life,* and the popular *Why Your Life Sucks and What You Can Do About It.* Alan is a contributing writer to the *New York Times* number one best-selling series Chicken Soup for the Soul. His books have been translated into twenty-one foreign languages.

Each month, Alan's column, *From the Heart,* is published in magazines internationally. His interviews and articles have been celebrated in numerous national and regional magazines.

Alan is a frequent guest on radio and television programs throughout the nation, including CNN, FOX News, CNBC, and many morning talk shows, and his seminars have been broadcast regularly on the Wisdom Channel. He is a faculty member at Omega Institute for holistic education. Alan has addressed personal-development organizations throughout the United States, Europe, Japan, Indonesia, the South Pacific, and South America. He also guides groups on excursions to sacred places such as Machu Picchu, Bali, and Egypt.

Alan resides in Maui, Hawaii, where he conducts retreats in life mastery.

LEARN MORE WITH ALAN COHEN

If you have enjoyed and found value in *Relax into Wealth,* you are invited to explore Alan Cohen's in-person or online seminars:

Daily Inspirational Quotes and Monthly E-Newsletter: Receive an uplifting quote daily via e-mail and Alan's monthly newsletter containing inspiring stories, recommendations, and updates on Alan's latest events, new books, and other offerings.

Online Courses: Receive a lesson each day via e-mail for one month and participate in a teleseminar (class via telephone). Subjects include: *Relax into Wealth; Building Great Relationships; The Time of Your Life;* and *Handle with Prayer.*

The Mastery Training: A six-day residential retreat at a beautiful location, to reconnect with yourself, tap into your passion, clarify your next step, and receive personal feedback and support from Alan to become all that you can be. The Mastery Training is currently offered in Sedona, Maui, and Fiji.

Personal Mentorship: Study closely with Alan and receive direct guidance to make successful life choices. Monthly personal coaching, small group retreat, and a committed connection between you, Alan, and like-minded people, to enable you to shine in every aspect of your life.

To register or receive more information on the above:

Visit: www.alancohen.com
E-mail: info@alancohen.com
Phone: (800) 568-3079
(808) 572-0001 (outside U.S.)
(808) 572-1023 (fax)
or write to:
Alan Cohen Publications
P.O. Box 835
Haiku, HI 96708
U.S.A.